IN FLUX

Trans and Gender-Diverse Reflections and Imaginings

IN FLUX

Trans and Gender-Diverse Reflections and Imaginings

Edited by Alex Nichols, David Azul,
Nick Lawson, The Swamp System
and Urszula Dawkins

THOUSAND THREADS PRESS | MELBOURNE

First published in 2022.

This book came into being following writing initiatives by Melbourne collectives A Thousand Threads: Stories of Us and Spilling the T Collective and is published by Thousand Threads Press. Email: hello@thousandthreadspress.com.au

We acknowledge that the land we all live and work on is stolen land. We pay our respects to the traditional owners, Elders past and present and emerging leaders.

NATIONAL LIBRARY OF AUSTRALIA

A catalogue record for this book is available from the National Library of Australia

ISBN: 978-0-6454294-2-8

Book design: Urszula Dawkins
Cover image: paki aoraki pehi, *Daddy Mase—Rarohenga*

This project is supported through the Maribyrnong City Council Community Grants Program.

Produced at River Studios, West Melbourne.

CITY OF MELBOURNE

CREATIVE SPACES

Acknowledgement of country

We acknowledge the First Peoples of this nation as the traditional owners of country throughout Australia. We recognise their ongoing connection to culture and country as custodians of the land and lore keepers of the oldest living culture, and we pay our respects to Elders past and present and to emerging leaders. We also pay our respects to First Nations people who contributed to this anthology.

These writings were composed on many different lands. We humbly acknowledge the Dja Dja Wurrung, Gulidjan, Boonwurrung, Wathaurong and Wurundjeri Woiwurrung peoples of the Kulin nation; the Dharug and Gadigal people of the Eora nation; the Yuggera people of the Meanjin nation; the Whadjuk people of the Noongar nation; and the Awabakal of the Muloobinba nation.

Sovereignty was never ceded and a treaty never negotiated. All the lands that comprise the nation of Australia were taken by force. The rights of Aboriginal people remain under-recognised, and in many ways the project of colonisation continues today.

May we remember how our oppressions and struggles are interconnected and stand alongside our First Nations comrades in the fight for justice.

CONTENTS

Introduction 11

A note to readers 17

Wings
Adele Aria 23

It was so much easier when we could just say US and THEM (Or, the things they say when they don't know who you are)
Hester J. Rook 25

No shame in womanhood
Kai Ash 29

Notes on poetry (A poem)
Sadie St James 35

Self-titled
Sadie St James 45

All of me is a pronoun
a. t. green 47

My gender is like two rivers
Jes Layton 51

Multiple choice
Madison Godfrey 59

Never coming out
Adele Aria 61

The first transgendered housewife
Shea Martin 63

Bin beauty
a. t. green 69

Marilyn
Louis Blake 71

Home
Nick Lawson 75

Cotton
Nick Lawson 77

The country in me
Adrik Kemp 81

The standard you walk past
Bron 'Richo' Richardson 87

Timberwolf
Isabelle Quilty 97

The vampire in the house
Rowan Heath 101

Happiness
Hailey McKenzie 109

Uplander
Eliot Jane Walton 115

The secret of ethr
Alex Lee 123

Open poem to [redacted], MP
Tobi Evans 131

Transrage (Or, anger is an investment in each other)
Madison Moffat, The Swamp System, Alex Lee 135

The drop
Sarah L 139

Fragmented mess
The Swamp System 145

Self-care trilogy
David Azul 153

Indelible
Jordie Slonim 159

In the absence of presence
Jordie Slonim 163

Love and other things (from the archives)
Nick Lawson 171

De l'espoir pour les communautés LGBTIQ africaines (Hope for African LGBTIQ communities)
Kashindi Shabani Gady 179

做你想做的人
(Zuò nǐ xiǎng zuò de rén/Be who you want to be)
Tiff Tan and anonymous collaborators 183

Sugar into syrup
Finnley Stirling 189

In unheard-of places
Hester J. Rook 191

Lions, tigers and bears
Son Vivienne 193

Corporeal
Shreya Tekumalla 201

Working late
Jules Joy 207

Re-emergence
Mohammad Taha 213

Ethereal release from form
Madison Moffat 217

Excerpt from 'The graphene prayer'
Geosmin Turpin 223

Noble maiden
Patterson Rainbird-Webb 225

like cryings
Elwin Schok 227

completeness
Elwin Schok 229

Afterword 231

The contributors 232

Thank you… 241

About this project 243

Image pages

Page 34, Sadie St James; page 46, Nick Lawson; pages 52–57, Jes Layton; page 70, Louis Blake; pages 78–79, Nick Lawson; page 122, Alex Lee; pages 144 and 152, David Azul; pages 162, 164, 166 and 168, Jordie Slonim; pages 177 and 206, Nick Lawson.

Text fragments throughout by Nick Lawson.

INTRODUCTION

We made this book as an artefact—something we could hold in our hands and say: 'These are our words'.

Although most of the pieces are individually authored, many were written alongside other folks in peer workshopping spaces. Even those written in the archetypical 'room of one's own' were enabled by connecting with the cultural production of other trans and gender-diverse (TGD) people. As such, this collection is driven not thematically but by a constellation of people and ideas in this historical moment.

In Flux has emerged from a recent upswell in gender-diverse community building, especially in Victoria. Here, increased government funding has powered services and cultural activities throughout the early years of the COVID pandemic. In 2019, legislation was passed to allow TGD people to change the sex marker on their birth certificate without surgery; a new community TGD health organisation increased accessibility to gender affirmation services; and Transgender Victoria launched its peer support program, funding dozens of community projects. Overall, there is a sense of increased visibility and mainstream acceptance.

2022 is eight years after *Time* magazine announced 'The transgender tipping point' with a cover feature on actress and activist, Laverne Cox. Her words describe the feelings of even more people today:

> *[M]ore and more trans people want to come forward and say, 'This is who I am.' … More of us are living visibly and pursuing our dreams visibly, so people can say, 'Oh yeah, I know someone who is trans.' When people have points of reference that are humanizing, that demystifies difference.*[1]

---

[1] https://time.com/135480/transgender-tipping-point/

In Flux forms part of this new wave of stories, but it is also intended as an intervention. The subtitle to the *Time* article is 'America's next civil rights frontier', placing it within a 'progress' narrative—the forward march of history from darkness to light. 'The trans person has arrived' is the message announced by Cox's confident gaze, perfect poise and elegant outfit. She is easily embraced by the mainstream as 'one of us, after all'. But the entangling of the trans person in the dream of liberalism denies our histories and our difference.

Generations of trans activists have fought to make space not only for these new conversations but for the very words they are spoken in. 'Trans' has evolved from the once pathologising terms 'transsexual' and 'transvestite', both of which have featured in the *Diagnostic and Statistical Manual of Mental Disorders* (DSM). Trans is not just the latest term in the rainbow family of identities. It bears within it histories of stigmatisation and marginalisation and struggles for self-determination. Moreover, even in the current era of trans rights, most gender-diverse lives are not lived inside the fantasy of upward mobility, as access to rights and privileges (e.g., education, a living wage and freedom from incarceration) is dictated by the disciplinary regimes of postcolonising, neoliberal democracy.

As much as we need the cover of *Time* magazine, we need space to tell our stories on our own terms. In this context, community-led publishing is crucial, giving gender-diverse folks opportunities for publication and control over their own storytelling. We need room for experiment and inquiry, and we need spaces to work together in order to keep figuring out what trans was, is and can be.

The title of our collection names a few different things. 'Flux' comes from the Latin *fluxus*, meaning 'flow'—so to be 'in flux' is to be flowing, moving, changing. This does not express uncertainty about who we are, nor, necessarily, an ever-shifting relation to our gender. Rather, it points to how trans is reconfiguring everyone's understandings of gender and personhood. As Jack Halberstam reminds us, trans 'constitutes a radically new knowledge about the experience of being in a body and can be the basis for very different ways of seeing the world'.[2]

In early usage, 'flux' also referred to an excess of bodily fluids. We wish to honour how the delicious messiness of bodies is part of the lived experience of many trans and gender-diverse folk.

Finally, an 'influx' is a different kind of flow: the arrival of a large number of people. Few of us 'arrive' as celebrities, but we *are* gathering collective force.

In Flux is an eclectic collection by diverse writers. Its geographical starting point was the municipality of Maribyrnong, in Naarm/Melbourne's inner west, and from there the authors fan out across Melbourne, Victoria and Australia, with two contributions from as far west as Africa. The writers all share lived experience of gender non-conformity and a wish to be read beside other gender-diverse folk. We cannot presume to speak for them, and the meanings of each work remain open to individual readers, but for those who want it, we signpost some possible themes.

One topic addressed here—though by no means the 'main' one—is 'gender' as a term of inquiry. Gender is a scheme for making ourselves and our worlds legible and coherent. TGD people are obliged to continually renegotiate liveable spaces. Our attention is drawn again and again to what it means to be a person with others, and *how* this 'being-a-person-ness'—which many take for granted—is actually made up of cultural norms. 'What *is* it?' is a question faced by many gender-diverse folk. Beyond the binary of 'man or woman' is another distinction: human or freak. In this book, Rowan Heath explores this monstrousness in 'The vampire in the house', while a. t. green's 'Bin beauty' and Hester J. Rook's two poems reclaim the freak with glamour, glitter and tenderness. Writing allows us to inquire into the terms of our dehumanisation.

Other writers turn gendered categories back on themselves. a. t. green's 'All of me is a pronoun' gives us iterations of he, she and they before insisting they're '…done/Making/This/Easy'. Madison Godfrey's 'Multiple choice' ends with 'My gender is none

---

[2] J. Halberstam (2016). 'Trans*—Gender transitivity and new configurations of body, history, memory and kinship', in *Parallax 22*(3), 366–375.

of the above.'. In 'No shame in womanhood', Kai Ash first declares what's great about 'a proud woman with hairy legs', but follows, '…that would be fine, good even, but for one glaring problem: I am not a woman.' Jes Layton refuses the 'either/or' of gender in graphic form, while Finnley Stirling moves from encounters with 'mainstream femininity' to 'the beauty of my otherness'. These writers redefine gender terms to create different understandings of what our culture 'knows' gender to be.

Life writing shows us the microstruggles borne by minorities as they come up against determinants and expectations embedded in language itself—the he/she of gender; racialisation; ablism. It can explore identity's arising—its making and often its multiplicity—in dialogue with varied social and discursive contexts.

Some of the pieces in this collection invite us into the everyday, tracking the constant *becoming* of ordinary life, leavened with tender emotion. Adele Aria's 'Wings' and Nick Lawson's 'Love and other things' speak of desire, from morning breath to fragile hearts. Sadie St James's 'Notes on Poetry' situates the writer's reflections in intimacy with trees, bugs, birds and leaves.

Other works explore the intersection of gender diversity, kinship and culture. Tiff Tan's 'Be who you want to be', Hailey McKenzie's 'Happiness', Sarah L's 'The drop', Patterson Rainbird-Webb's 'Noble maiden' and Shreya Tekumalla's 'Corporeal' all explore family relationships and the movements and losses that occur both within and without family structures.

Who we are and who we can be changes depending where we are. 'Corporeal', Son Vivienne's 'Lions, tigers and bears' and Adrik Kemp's 'The country in me'—written on behalf of a trans person unable to name himself publicly—are also journeys, with the protagonists' possibilities unfolding differently as their location changes. Through such changes, we live in our bodies, wherever we are and whoever we are with. Louis Blake and Madison Moffat trace with particular humour and heart how the joys of embodiment sit alongside aversion, ambivalence and dysphoria.

Just a few works in this collection present clearly as fiction; notably, they are all in some sense speculative. Jules Joy's 'Working late' evokes gothic horror, while Isabelle Quilty's 'Timberwolf' reads as high fantasy. Mohammad Taha's 'Re-emergence' seems both distant and close, skirting between truth and make-believe, while Shea Martin invents a surreal girls' club drawn in glitz, glam and pop-culture references. More obviously 'speculative' are 'The drop,' Eliot Jane Walton's 'Uplander' and Alex Lee's 'The secret of ethr', which immerse us into fantastical pasts and dystopian futures where gender regimes dominate and dissidents fight back—dramatising the tensions of our own system. They ask: Can constructing fictive worlds enable us to open up our present as well as imagine different futures?

Poetry and poetic prose can also provide much-needed space for experiment—to find and test the new language needed to express our embodiment as TGD folk. Jordie Slonim, Geosmin Turpin and Elwin Schok, among others, pull language back and forth to achieve their purpose, viscerally exploring relationships, examining inner processes and threading words into unexpected turns of fragment/phrase to capture the physicality and feeling of being embodied and in their worlds. The Swamp System, too, share their inner worlds through the multiple voices of their being.

In many countries trans lives are increasingly lived amid ideological battlegrounds. Tobi Evans's 'Open poem' and a collective piece, 'Transrage', critique how public political rhetorics position trans people, while David Azul's and Richo Richardson's pieces track their authors' encounters with the medical and military institutions. Kashindi Shabani Gady's 'Hope for LGBTIQ African communities' describes a different political landscape, taking us through a week in the life of an LGBT activist in Bukavu, Democratic Republic of Congo. The members of their community and organisation, Savie Asbl, face overt hostility and violence—including from their own government—and so cannot live openly as queer, trans or gender-diverse.

In Flux: Trans and Gender-Diverse Reflections and Imaginings is both a celebration and a record of our shared creativity and community building. It is also the sharing of a critical energy, joining 'I' to 'you'.

'Tell me, so we can remember together'—our epigraph, from Sadie St James, speaks in the voice of one writer to another, but it is also an invitation to the reader. We ask that you open your hearts to our words, so that together we may re-compose the worlds we live in.

Alex Nichols and Urszula Dawkins, Naarm, November 2022

A note to readers

These stories and poems were written by people with a range of different life experiences, and what's empowering for one reader may be distressing for another. This list flags themes which some readers may find upsetting. Please take care as you read.

Anatomical or slang words for body parts: 'Marilyn', 'Open poem…'

Dehumanising ideas (transphobic, misogynist, sexist, racist, ableist): 'The first transgendered housewife', 'The standard you walk past', 'The vampire in the house', The secret of ethr', 'Transrage', 'The drop', 'Hope for African LGBTIQ communities'

Drug use: 'It was so much easier…', 'Bin beauty', 'Lions, tigers and bears'

Dysphoria: 'No shame in womanhood'

Family rejection: 'The country in me', 'The drop', 'Be who you want to be'

Homophobic or transphobic slurs: 'The standard you walk past', 'Ethereal release from form'

Hospitalisation and medical procedures: 'Marilyn', The country in me', 'The vampire in the house', 'Self-care trilogy'

Menstruation: 'Cotton'

Military: 'The standard you walk past'

Psychological distress and trauma: 'Fragmented mess', 'Self-care trilogy', 'Indelible', 'Ethereal release from form'

Sexual abuse: 'Lions, tigers and bears'

Suicide or suicidal ideation: 'Notes on poetry', 'Never coming out', 'The standard you walk past', 'Ethereal release from form', Excerpt from 'The graphene prayer'

Violence: 'No shame in womanhood', 'Hope for African LGBTIQ communities', Excerpt from 'The graphene prayer'

For those who have come before us, those who are still to come
and those who are here now. Who fight for us and themselves.
So that they, and we, may live better lives.

Tell me, so we can remember together

WINGS

Adele Aria

Wake her up
Wild hair held in a line of drool
tugging the corners of her mouth
Defiantly smirking
at morning breath that mouthwash and toothpaste
only make gums ache
Feel edges of cloudiness
mingle with dissipating dreams
before his outside world
presses in with demands.

Wait for her to uncoil
Untuck from a corner she was made to occupy
to fumble with the clasp of a bra
Lovers promise their experience
instead to fumble and grumble to uncover
a body they don't please
Donning armour of stories and music
the glow of a phone lights her scowl
her skirt mocking attempts
to exist unsullied by scrutiny.

IT WAS SO MUCH EASIER WHEN WE COULD JUST SAY US AND THEM

Or, the things they say when they don't know who you are

Hester J. Rook

They say:

I just don't get it.
It's fine, I guess, but pansexuality?
They're making up words out of nothing.
I just don't want to ask.
Genderqueer? No, that's going too far.
I was going to make this *joke* but I knew you'd be offended.
I'm just not *comfortable* with queer stuff
(laughing).

But they do not know I live the most beautiful life.

I have:

1. gifs of Natalie Dormer

2. the fingersting memories of last Saturday, holding the hip of a woman as she dances and turns and kisses me newly on the mouth. The swell of a room full of *us*, lipstick against the microphone and the full-belly swoop as we merge in flight.

Brendan Maclean in fake-fur red as guts and songs that bucket around my head like prayer

3. kisses against mouths that remind me of beautiful things, like strawberries

4. those photos of Tessa Thompson, hair braided into a whip (you know, the ones that stopper your throat)

5. the knowledge burnt through of my longest love's curls on my lips. The twine of her voice on the phone, photos of her sun-slept and warm as summer nights as she soaks up stars somewhere (for now) unreachable

6. slices of ripe persimmon on a chopping board and fat black grapes in the sun, each sweet and soft and tense until the rind bursts under my teeth; the gentle line of fingernails against my palm

7. shine-stung tiles under my knees as my housemate buzzes my undercut, as we unspill our hearts in warm baths in places rimed with autumn, as we delve into our naked chests and turn ourselves into imperfect words to be kept safe, and only safe

8. the butterfly tangle of limbs under covers and whispered secrets and fears and traumas that in summary tell me only *I TRUST YOU*

9. *Oceans 8*, and therefore Cate Blanchett in a sequined suit whenever I damn well please (let's be real though, it's the motorbike scene that chokes me every time)

10. the line of her cheekbone under my thumb

11. (to my right) my friend high as fuck sprawled across my lap, their hands clutching mine, (to my left) the friend I will later kiss resting against the backdrop of the spilled-light city, my community pulsing on a dance floor

12. car rides humming with *Dirty Computer*, all of us singing badly and loudly and the sun reaching greedy fingers over the dashboard, dirt crusting our boots

13. messages shaped like questions, messages like 'I would like to kiss you on the face', questions which swan-dive down my throat, unpeel my skin, settle right down into the ends of my toes

14. her hair curled through my bed, her coat as company while I am ill, my cat curled up in corduroy and purring gentle and loud all at once

15. those gifs of Natalie Dormer, remember? In a hammock, eating an apple. Fuck.

> I have the held moments, each exquisite and new and
> precious; the shy reach towards hands
> the perfect awkward explicit questions.
> how do I not make you hurt?
> you are beautiful and I would not see you hurt

I could fall for you, but I would not have you hurt.

People are all too willing to tell us who we are and deny our magic

NO SHAME IN WOMANHOOD

Kai Ash

I don't like pink.

I wear my hair short.

I don't shave my legs or underarms.

I wear loose, masculine clothing.

I don't wear makeup.

None of these things excludes me from womanhood.

No, what excludes me from womanhood is this: I am not a woman. Though I look like one.

There is a sensation called *dysphoria*, though I prefer the words *disjuncture*, *disunion* or *dissonance*. For some, it is a loud and violent thing, driving them to take action against their own flesh. For me, it is quieter. It is a lack of recognition when I look in the mirror. It is a difficulty with holding the concept of my own body in my mind. It is a conscious, and unconscious, refusal to acknowledge my physical reality.

I did not choose to experience this sensation, and I was intimately familiar with it decades before I knew it had a name. Learning the word and learning others' experiences of it simply gave me a language to describe my own.

When I am a very small child, I meet dysphoria. It arrives in my world all of a sudden as I jump into the bath with my siblings and cousins and begin to note oddly consistent differences. While every body seems completely unique to me at this age—different colours, different shapes, different textures—I'm beginning to notice that there are some differences that fall under larger headings: ones marked Female and Male.

It gets worse later. My body grows, but my brothers' grow more. They are taller, their shoulders broader, their faces pimplier and their scents sharper. As our bodies diverge in shape and texture, so to do our realities. We are treated differently, and we treat one another differently in turn.

I look in the mirror, and it is now clearly a young woman looking back at me. This realisation is painful, and distinctly dysphoric, but I tell myself that I am done with pretence. There is a young woman in my reflection, and it is time for me to accept that reality. So I do. Begrudgingly.

In psychology textbooks, autistic people are often described as having 'black and white thinking' and, according to many of my old teachers and associates, I am no exception. I disagree with this assessment but acknowledge that I do have a tendency towards firm and fast decision-making. For example, when I am a teenager, I choose to see myself as a woman on the basis of what I see in the mirror. What I feel inside, how I think, my very sense of self is nothing in the face of the incontrovertible physical evidence before me. I see a female body, and so I say to myself: 'You are a woman.'

My commitment to womanhood is helped along by my favourite film, Pedro Almodóvar's *All About My Mother.* There is a tribute at the end of the film, a dedication to mothers and women everywhere, including '*los hombres que actúan y se convierten en mujeres*'—'the men who act and become women'.

I see myself in this dedication. I am a man, becoming a woman.

I am blessed to be surrounded by glorious women. Role models of every variety. They are in my family, my community and the books I devour to better understand the world.

Like many autistic people, I often struggle to understand why people behave the way that they do, particularly when they are in groups. As a young person, I rely heavily on books and stories for insight and explanation. I read and I learn and I apply my new knowledge to my life.

I learn that I can be a woman without following every rule of femininity. Perfume, makeup, high heels—none of these things are compulsory. There are costs to not conforming, but they are not particularly high in my mind. I will never be a social being, so low-level social ostracism is a minor penalty.

But I do conform to an extent. For years, I shave my legs and under my arms. I wear tinted sunscreen as a nod towards make-up and buy all my clothes from the female section of the store.

I am called lesbian and dyke without ever kissing a woman, or even holding one's hand. I am invited into queer spaces and dismissed from straight ones without any overt action required on my part. I simply am, and the spaces open and close accordingly.

My favourite moments, the ones that send fizzing joy through my body, are the 'accidents', when strangers slip and call me 'he' and 'sir' and 'mate'. Though they are hastily corrected to 'she' and 'ma'am' and 'luv', I collect these brief moments of euphoria and carry them close. They are my guilty pleasure.

I study gender studies and attend readings of Eve Ensler's *The Vagina Monologues*. I collect feminist treatises and organise my thoughts around what it means to be female-bodied in this world.

It is at university that I first properly meet the word *transgender*, but it is closely followed by a showing of the film *Boys Don't Cry*, which depicts a trans man being raped and murdered. Needless to say, I am not enticed by the idea of being so brutalised. I turn away and put it from my mind.

'I am a woman,' I tell myself, looking at the body in the mirror. This is my reality, and I accept it.

I like being a strong woman. Few want to be my friend, but many express their admiration for my confidence.

'I wish I could be like you,' they say.

'Never change,' they tell me.

But meeting other strong women, and listening to them speak, is confusing. They are different from me. They don't seem to struggle with their own flesh the way I do. When we discuss bodies and discomfort, they speak about weight concerns, or the need to conform to a distinctly white feminine ideal. In these discussions, they take their womanhood as a given, not something they have to struggle and strive for. They are women, and they know it.

I am not good at feeling like a woman. I forget. And then I have to remind myself, which I do by standing in front of the mirror, naked, and focusing my attention on all my most womanly features.

But my mind is wily. It will acknowledge the wide girth of my hips, and the thinness of my shoulders, but then it will point out that my eyes come straight from my father's face, that my nose is surely most comparable to my uncle's, and that the shape of my feet is distinctly male, as only the men in my family have such low arches.

My body becomes a collection of mismatched parts, some female, some male, and my sense of dysphoria grows. Until I reach my thirties and it finally bursts.

In the year leading up to my official Coming Out as Trans moment, I experience a lot of angst. I feel like I am a traitor to feminism. That I am failing all those strong women I so admire, including my own mother, by taking this step. I feel like I am suggesting that one cannot be strong and confident *and* a woman. I feel like I owe it to girls and women everywhere to keep going as I am.

'Don't ever change,' I have been told, over and over again, by friends and strangers. It is meant as a compliment, I think, but the words smother me.

'Don't change,' they tell me, and what I hear is that they want me to continue being the one who smashes feminine norms.

They want me to be the proud woman with hairy legs and a gives-no-shits attitude. They want me to show the world that there's more than one way to be a woman.

And that would be fine, good even, except for one glaring problem: I am not a woman.

It is fitting that my Coming Out Moment takes place in the bathroom, standing in front of the mirror, just me and my reflection, once again staring each other down. In the end, it plays out like Princess Leia farewelling Han Solo in *Star Wars: The Empire Strikes Back.*

I say to my reflection: 'I am trans.'

And my reflection responds: 'I know.'

And it really is that simple, though perhaps that perception is just another example of my so-called 'black and white thinking'.

I tell my partner-at-the-time, then my family, my friends and work, and finally the government for a name change. There are hiccups and stumbles and low points, but mostly an overwhelming sense of relief and rightness.

When I turn 31, I celebrate my first birthday ever as a man, and it is a homecoming. For decades I have been trying to be what I am not, and now I am free to simply be.

I am still surrounded by glorious women, in my family, in my community and in my books. Some of my old heroes I have had to leave behind, and that process has been a painful one, but I try not to dwell on those disappointments. For every anti-trans 'feminist' I once admired, there are a myriad of old and new voices to treasure.

All About My Mother is still one of my favourite films, but now I see myself less in Almodóvar's dedication to all the men who become women, and more in the text that appears on the back cover of the DVD, and in the film's 1999 theatrical trailer: 'Part of every man…is a woman.'

NOTES ON POETRY
A poem

Sadie St James

Poetry is intoxicating for a hyperactive brain;

because it is done when it is done
It's harder to share, but it contains within itself all of its own pieces
Poetry asks what your day was like,

but not in the way that a friend does
It asks you instead to describe what your bus ride home was like
What the sun looked like as it broke the horizon
Not at the beginning, but at the end
Poetry speaks to the skin, it filters out everything that
isn't beautiful
It finds beauty where you thought there was none

It interrogates in a way that journalling can't,
In a way that no grandiose tale of fiction can contain

It weaves fantasy and the senses

together with personality and emotions,
It calls out to be felt again and again
You cannot read it too many times, only familiarise yourself with it
The magic does not dwindle as it becomes a script
Poetry thrives in a sober mind just as much as an affected one
And although it is best spoken by a sober tongue, that does not
make any demands of the reader they cannot themselves
follow through

Because it looks deep inside
and says:
Yes, but what made you today?
Which events will you remember so vividly,
That you don't even need to write them down?
What will you need to be reminded of?
Poetry is the storyteller with a voice so familiar that even the blanks—

Are just negative space

So,
What *made* you today?
Tell me, so we can remember together
Show me,
So we know for next time

20 April 2022

18 March 2022

I climbed a gum today
I haven't climbed a tree in years,

should probably have started with a fig
But there was something so intoxicating about the thought
of climbing to the 'Highest point in Melbourne'

—and then some
As is so often the case, her surface was far less accommodating
than her frame
I gouged my hands, tore tiny chunks from bare feet
And almost wrecked my best pants

I would do it with all the vigour
Again and again
In jeans, from now on

Climbing a gum tree is an exercise in trust
For she staunchly refuses to make it easy
You have only yourself to ask:
How far will my body stretch?

—further than you think, but not THAT far

How steady is my grip?

—as firm as your resolve,
as reliable as the Moon and Sun

How far can I fall?

—no further than you have come,
for better or worse.

Because if you turn back too soon, you miss the chance to rest
in her crook
To realise she could survive more than you ever thought possible
You miss the chance to believe the same of yourself.

22 March 2022

I went for a walk to get caught in the rain
And I saw a jasmine bush in my front yard
Or—I smelled her
I hesitate to believe she could have sprung up overnight
But how else could I have overlooked her for so long?
I choose to think you left her there
A reminder
That I don't always have to go somewhere to find you
To be with you
I know you
—Knew you
And so perhaps you hid her from me
Until the moment I most needed to know

That looking backwards isn't always bad
I mean, isn't that how you find your way home?

7 April 2022

A short story

I was watching a bug on the glass
Wondering if I was seeing the brown underside of a black bug

or the black underside of a brown bug
She paused at the giant sticker emblazoned across the window
and I held my breath

I was watching a bug through the glass;
because as she ascended the vinyl mountain I never saw her again.

He is sitting by the back door, she enters
I don't know if they planned to meet on this bus, but their
destinations are the same

One below the steps, one above
Words that are not mine to interpret explain the divide

Twenty minutes later, the allure of a shared screen and a hand on a
shoulder obliterates it

This is their bus now, and when they leave we will all be
disconnected from one another once more

Why am I writing this?
Why am I crying?

I think because I feel like I never cherished my moments as a
lovestruck stranger enough
Or maybe,
Because I know I did.

29 May 2022

An autumn leaf was blown into my shirt
My irritation was interrupted, by the intimacy of the moment
As I turned and looked unsuccessfully for the tree from which it had come
The anonymous romanticism of the moment compelled me to make a souvenir of it
And suddenly it didn't matter that the shopping centre had lost power

I saw another leaf fall
Gliding gracefully through the air, vibrant red and eager to join the expansive carpet beneath
Her fall was interrupted by the hood of a car
I watched two successive vehicles crush her with their tyres
As I waited for a break to retrieve the body

I kept them both
To be polymerised and immortalised within the bindings of this book

I carry pieces of earth with me wherever I go now
Some are gifted, but others are borrowed
I brought back a quartz from the gorge near my house
Showed my life to her, asked for guidance
Looked at her and saw that the beautiful thing was the memory of the place
So I took her home

My river jasper has been asking to go home too
I don't know, maybe it's the memory of the place
It was a journey then and it's an odyssey now
It's a place I cannot go alone

But it's time I learned how to travel farther than my feet can carry me once more—
Time I allowed myself to dream bigger

4 June 2022

I used to go to sleep to the sound of the birds
These days, I wake up to it
There's not much to do that early
But go for a walk, and window-shop through 'Closed' signs

And listen
Listen to the birds
To the world waking up
It's winter now, though what that means these days is uncertain
All I know is that the spring chicks are losing their
fledgling plumage
And the birds are all traveling in twos
The dances may be done
The fights for a mate won
But the courtships have still barely begun

They are learning the world together
Finding a home to raise their young
How can it be?
It seems just yesterday you needed help to eat
Now you glide, climb and sing with ease
Soon, you will help someone else eat

And so as the nights get colder, and the days shorter
Each waking hour is precious
Each restful moment is vital
And on Sundays
I rise with the birds
And sing with my flock.
I think,
I might go for a walk

23 June 2022

You still smell like a new book
I feel like you would have wanted to smell like an old book
Wouldn't we all?
A fresh book smells like a waiting room before something underwhelming
But it also smells like a launch,
Without an author
Like a pile of fresh-pressed words
A table, empty before the room was

When I am gone, I will smell like brown paper and polymer glue
I will smell like a packed lunch and a craft table
Like a grocery delivery
An unassuming cover is imperative for people like us
We've spent too long being judged from the outside
Being more visible than we knew what to do with

I have been wading through all the things you left behind
And when I find myself floored by the similarities
I remember that post you made less than a year before you left
About how you finally wanted so much to stay

I'm sure I'm not the only one who always knew, that when you begged for your words to persevere even if you didn't
That it was a threat
Virginia's last poem was her note
And when I get into knives
Or unlock myself from a string of black pearls with the same awl I use to bind my books
I play chicken with myself,
Challenging life to hold more excitement than the car careening off the road.

3 August 2022

When I'm Gone

When I'm gone
Bring a picnic to the place I'm laid to rest
Choose a pleasant day
Don jackets; blankets, thermoses
Pack all the foods that I liked best

When I'm gone
Please read to me
The books I never finished; the ones I never shut up about
Tell me stories
Of all the things you grew up to be

When I'm gone
Come dance upon my grave
Smile and laugh and serenade
You don't have to be strong or stoic
There's no-one to see you be brave

When I'm gone
Ask what you miss, when you miss me
Remember all the things I left you with
And when you feel too alone to go on
Reach inside and kiss me

SELF-TITLED

Sadie St James

I spent the first 21 years of my life 'in flux'
Unable to settle on any solid form
These days, I sit firmly within the confines of certainty
My gender exists outside the binary
As a trans woman, though, that's rarely up to me
I am trans, no footnote or appendix necessary
Transness will never have a monopoly on the disparity
Between expectations and reality
We are all non-Newtonian liquids
In a world intent on breaking promises
I am trans, and probably more sure of myself than you
If you feel the need to add some punctuation—
A period will do.

ALL OF ME IS A PRONOUN

a. t. green

All of me is a pronoun—

'he' is in my knees
kneeling
for you.

'she' is in my stubble
and lipstick.

'he' is dresses on a
Sunday afternoon.

'she' is tiny toes encased in
big
black
boots.

All of me is a pronoun—

clearly marked
so easy to carve up.

'she' is shaved head
'he' long flowing locks
'they' multi-hued mohawk.

All of me is a pronoun—

you asked me to define this for you
Don’t be surprised when I don’t
make this easy.

All of me is a pronoun—

‘he’ is getting loose in an alley with strangers and smiles
‘she’ is binder, strap-on and red wine in the evening
‘they’ lurks in the space between your moans
lapping up your desire.

All of me is a pronoun—

we can sweat off make-up
and binders
But can’t seem to sweat away the perceptions of strangers
Or the demands to make it visible
make it small
make it easy.

All of me is a pronoun—

‘they’ gets stuck in your throat
You choke on it
‘cause there are only two of everything—
right?
Nothing exists in between
Make this easy
make this easy.

All of me is a pronoun—

‘they’ joins a punk band
takes up too much space
and swells their belly with testosterone.

All of me is a pronoun—

but you don’t get to decide what that means.

My swagger is femme
the softness of my soul is MASC
Do not fight me on definitions.

All of me is a pronoun—

I'm the inhabitant of this crater of hope made flesh
Why can't I name the contents
with loving rage?

All of me is a pronoun—

But I'm done
Making
This
Easy.

MY GENDER IS LIKE TWO RIVERS

Jes Layton

I'VE ALWAYS SWUNG BETWEEN PRESENTING MORE MASCULINE AND PRESENTING MORE FEMININE, EQUALLY AND ALWAYS; A BOY OR A GIRL
WHEN ASKED I SAY THAT MY GENDER IS LIKE TWO RIVERS
RUNNING INTO THE SAME OCEAN
GENDERFLUID IN THE MOST LITERAL WAY
THAT'S WHAT I TELL PEOPLE. AND YET, I STILL DON'T ENTIRELY KNOW WHAT I MEAN BY THAT.

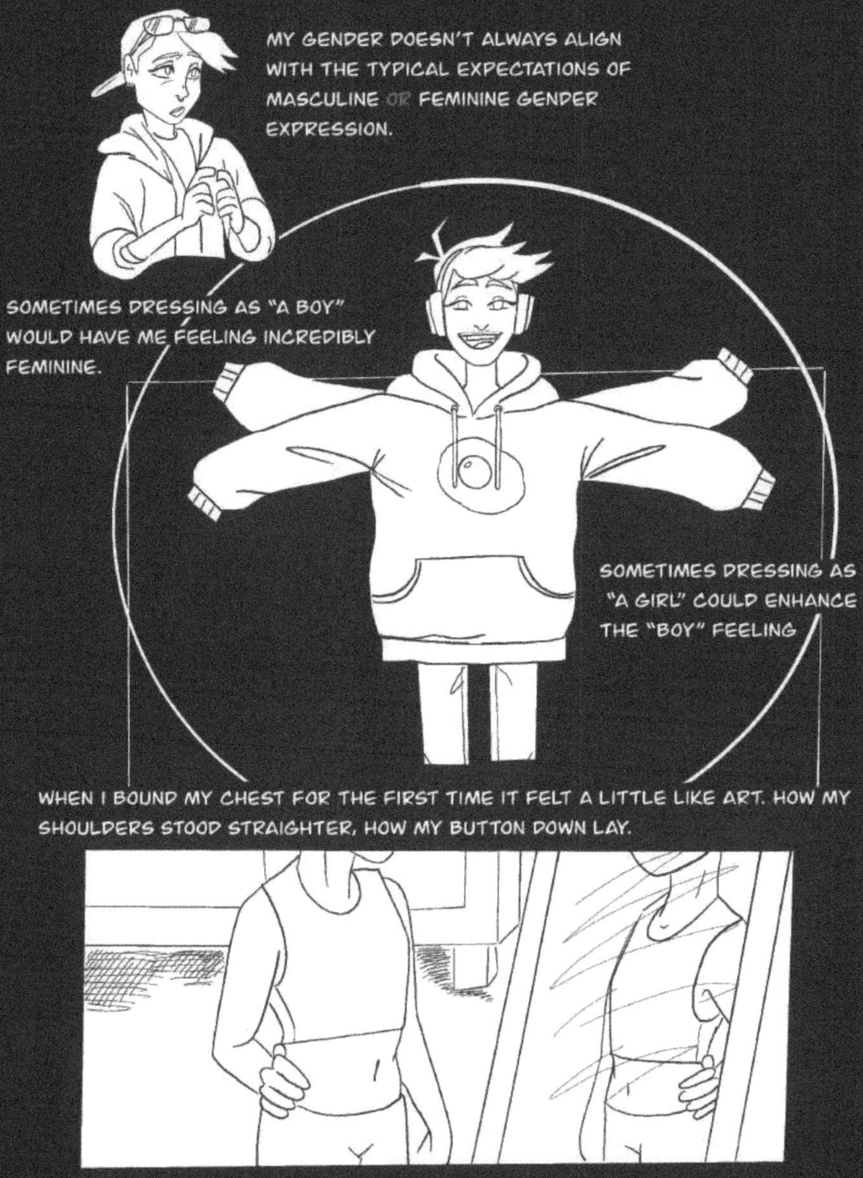
MY GENDER DOESN'T ALWAYS ALIGN WITH THE TYPICAL EXPECTATIONS OF MASCULINE OR FEMININE GENDER EXPRESSION.
SOMETIMES DRESSING AS "A BOY" WOULD HAVE ME FEELING INCREDIBLY FEMININE.
SOMETIMES DRESSING AS "A GIRL" COULD ENHANCE THE "BOY" FEELING
WHEN I BOUND MY CHEST FOR THE FIRST TIME IT FELT A LITTLE LIKE ART. HOW MY SHOULDERS STOOD STRAIGHTER, HOW MY BUTTON DOWN LAY.

AT TIMES, SPEAKING ABOUT THE PARTS OF MY BODY IN THE CONTEXT OF MY GENDER IS LIKE WAVING TO SOMEONE WHO YOU REALISE WAS ACTUALLY WAVING TO SOMEONE ELSE BEHIND YOU

BUT NOW, WEARING A BINDER MAKES ME FEEL STRONG AND FREE IN SOME WAY. SIMILAR TO THE LITTLE TITTY WIGGLING OF A LOOSE NIPPLE IN A BAGGY T-SHIRT

I LOOK AT MYSELF NOWADAYS AND SEE A MYTHIC FIGURE STANDING THERE

A MODERN APHRODITUS

OR IPHIS

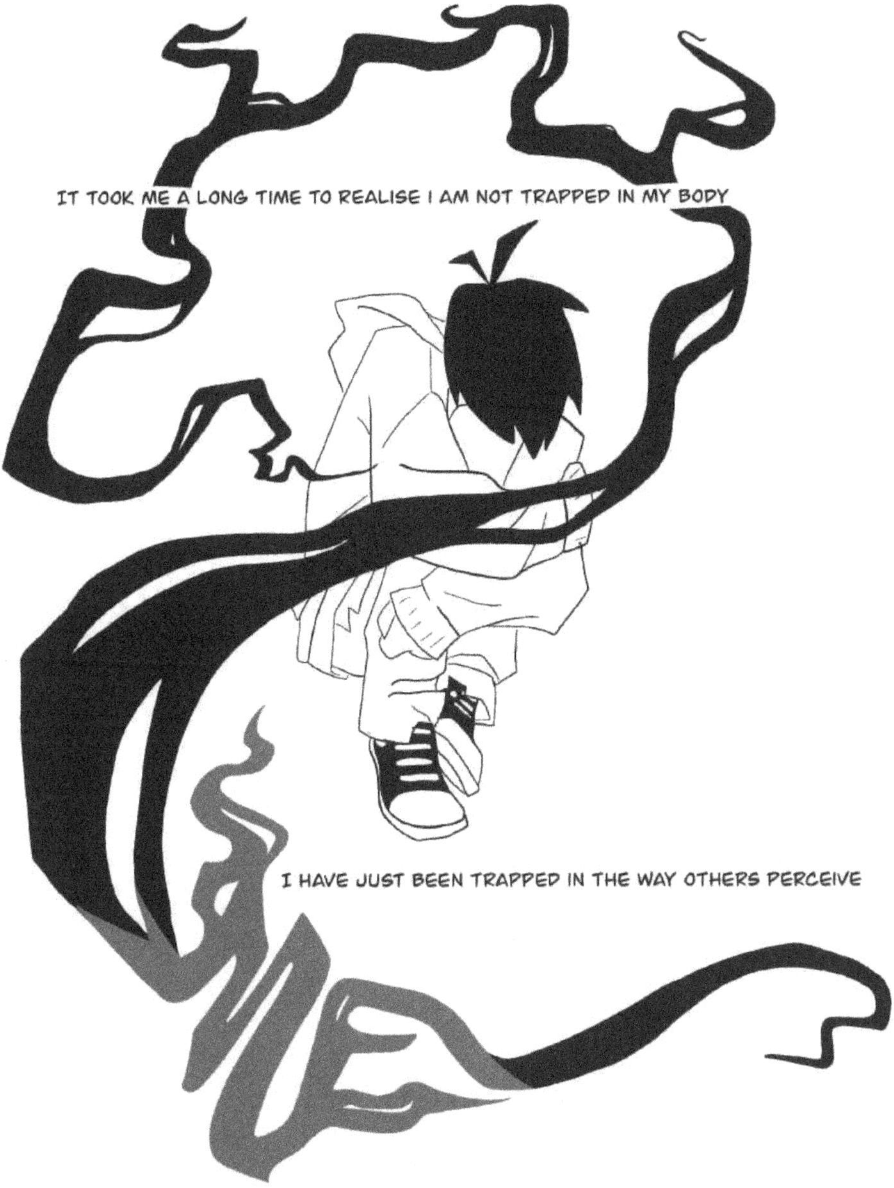
IT TOOK ME A LONG TIME TO REALISE I AM NOT TRAPPED IN MY BODY
I HAVE JUST BEEN TRAPPED IN THE WAY OTHERS PERCEIVE

I KNOW NOW THAT THIS KNOWLEDGE IS SOME KIND OF POWERFUL
THAT DOESN'T MEAN I DON'T STILL HAVE QUESTIONS

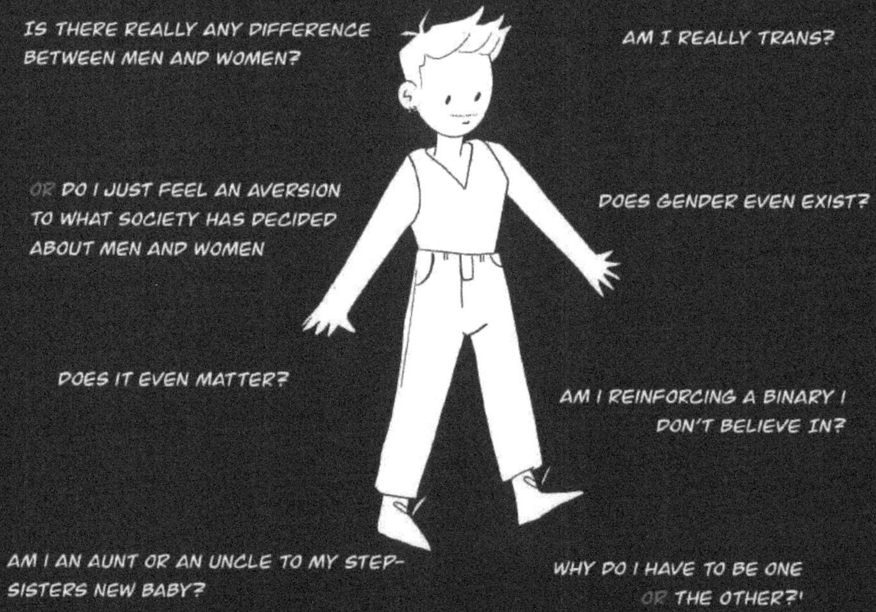
IS THERE REALLY ANY DIFFERENCE BETWEEN MEN AND WOMEN?
AM I REALLY TRANS?
OR DO I JUST FEEL AN AVERSION TO WHAT SOCIETY HAS DECIDED ABOUT MEN AND WOMEN
DOES GENDER EVEN EXIST?
DOES IT EVEN MATTER?
AM I REINFORCING A BINARY I DON'T BELIEVE IN?
AM I AN AUNT OR AN UNCLE TO MY STEP-SISTERS NEW BABY?
WHY DO I HAVE TO BE ONE OR THE OTHER?!

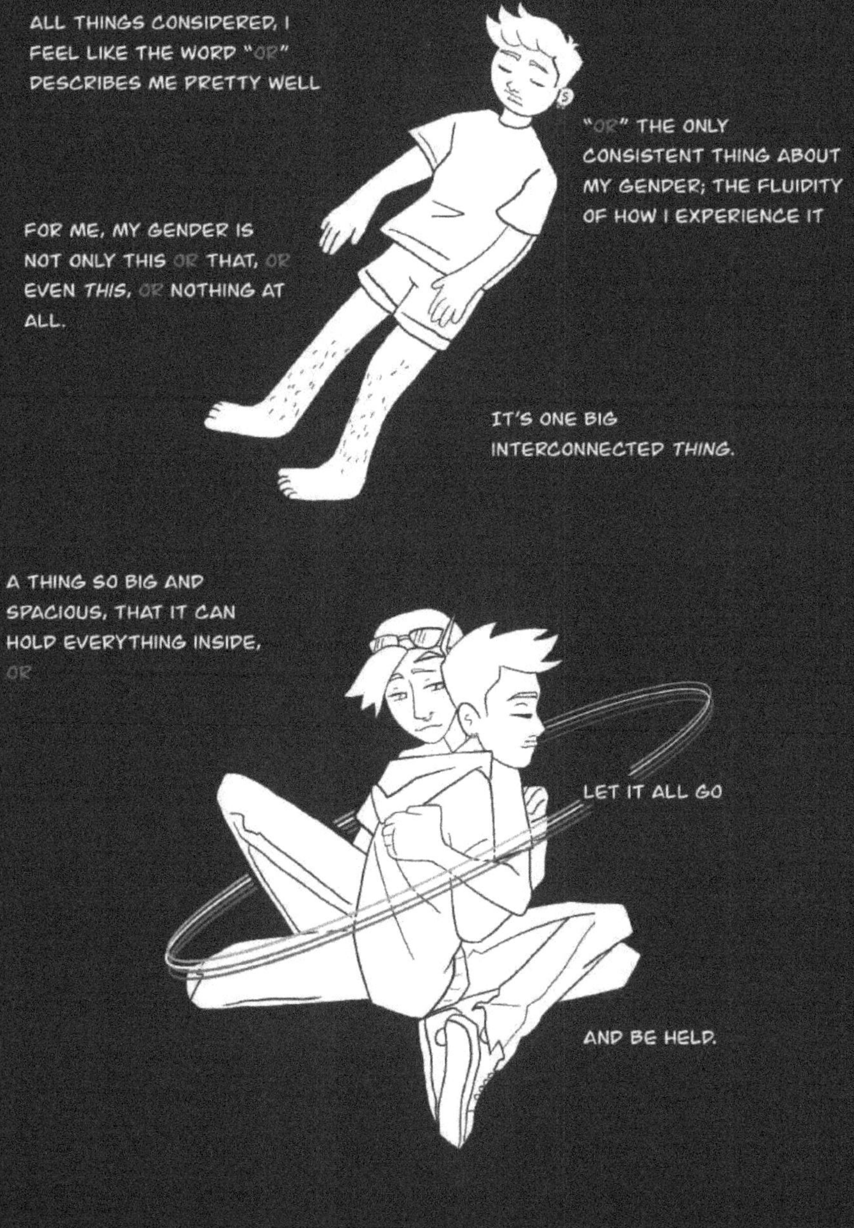
ALL THINGS CONSIDERED, I FEEL LIKE THE WORD "OR" DESCRIBES ME PRETTY WELL
"OR" THE ONLY CONSISTENT THING ABOUT MY GENDER; THE FLUIDITY OF HOW I EXPERIENCE IT
FOR ME, MY GENDER IS NOT ONLY THIS OR THAT, OR EVEN *THIS,* OR NOTHING AT ALL.
IT'S ONE BIG INTERCONNECTED *THING.*
A THING SO BIG AND SPACIOUS, THAT IT CAN HOLD EVERYTHING INSIDE, OR
LET IT ALL GO
AND BE HELD.

MULTIPLE CHOICE

Madison Godfrey

A.

My gender is a clown suit. Mostly it makes people smile but sometimes it makes people uncomfortable. Sometimes I paint the face my mother wore before she met my father. More often, I paint the face my father wore the first afternoon he loved my mother. My gender started writing jokes so it could stop being the joke. My gender turns up late to the children's birthday booking. My gender releases balloons by accident. My gender watches them float away, knowing this is the gentlest introduction to grief. My gender departs on a tiny bicycle. My gender sends an invoice.

B.

My gender is an outfit that Christina Aguilera wears in the 2010 film *Burlesque*. My gender feels sexy in tassels. My gender answers to no body. My gender grew up a country gal then became a big-city-cabaret-star with a hot bartender boyfriend. My gender is envious of Cher. Or, my gender is envious of women who age towards their womanhood, instead of away from it. My gender searches *does Cher have children*? My gender hates being called *a career woman*. My gender wants to make *Mum* a non-gendered term. My gender rehearses lines. My gender rehearses androgyny. My gender straddles a piano stool and glances over their shoulder towards an audience of actors. My gender is waiting for Cher to appear behind them in the mirror and apply eyeliner so precise it resembles a tightrope. My gender can belt a chorus after years of silence.

C.

My gender works at a nail salon owned by ghosts. My gender asks what colour you desire today, but all the bottles are named after people you met in the hallways of house parties. My gender files your fingertips into daggers. My gender moisturises your hands like a lover. My gender wants you to feel good about feeling good. My gender is a place where others learn their softness. My gender asks if you would like two coats of glitter.

D.

My gender sings their own lyrics at karaoke.

E.

My gender is none of the above.

NEVER COMING OUT

Adele Aria

In many ways
life in brief
signalled through
resonant bones
wavering joints
and pronouncements
by doctor
after sage
after
recast barber
only wanting hope—
or begging fragments.
Mourning
not knowing.

They choose
parts to celebrate
what not to see
palatable glories
to brag
silken blindfolds
Decorate dinner parties
in one-up games
acting out happiness
Waiting turn
feeling smug and relieved
their lot
shaped unlike
others

Losing battles
drawn lines
Spoken unheard
Their house
never home
With lens reshaping
a book always closed
not fully allowed
Chose what to be
to hold and uphold
value and measure
Select what to be
In terms
on hostile territory
Success is survival

Finally resting
mourning the masks
they ordered
and endorsed
No depth
angles or shadows
Dismissing
blurring lines
awkward whole

Staying safe enough
To Die
young.

THE FIRST TRANSGENDERED HOUSEWIFE

Shea Martin

A symphony for laying place cards. *This bitch must not sit next to this bitch, but these two bitches absolutely must be seated together.* Thirteen pewter bangles harmoniously clanging against one another. The gentle slosh of organic, bergamot handwash lubricating a de-plumed chicken. The sizzle of a curling iron loosening the glue that binds a Malaysian woman's hair to that of a native of our locale.

These women like to talk a big game, but I like great, big diamonds.

Adelaide. Her décolletage is beyond frosted, it's freezer-burned. A webbing of Swarovski crystals reaches beneath her shoulders and dives to meet the neckline of a champagne gown, woven onto her figure by that same ostentatious arachnid. Two small children dance behind her. They are insignificant. She sways on the spot, places her hand on her hip and bores a hole into your forehead with her joyless gaze.

I'm not your average Arcadian girl, my daughter only goes to the second-most-expensive school in the district.

Greta. This one is clad in burlap. Perhaps 'wrapped' would be more accurate. She looks like a burrito, or rather a woman with an uncomfortably dark tan housed within a burrito. She had requested to be barefoot, but the producers refused to allow it. Instead, she has removed her acrylic toenails in protest. The afore-mentioned daughter stands behind her in a black turtleneck and leather jodhpurs. You could be forgiven for thinking she had been adopted on a sojourn to Seoul, but she was born to two Caucasian parents here, in Arcadia.

The only thing I feed on is secrets, and sometimes a tiny, little bit of salami.

Misty. The mess of the group, clearly. Her hair is enormous. To say that it's full of secrets would be cheap, and also a lie. In fact, it is full of hairspray, gel, mousse, tulle, packing tape and, as she is yet to learn, her phone charger. It's difficult to discern exactly what she is wearing, as most of her avian body is obscured by an enormous clutch that she is only just able to carry with both of her tiny arms. Her smile is as wide as her little bobblehead, and it's real because she knows that this season, she isn't going to be the one on trial.

$

The girls are back in town. The girls have poured themselves over the three largest tables in a cafe that was very trendy about 18 months ago and are politely yelling to one another across the cafe floor. The girls are already drunk.

Do you know, I actually haven't been here since Melinda's 40th?

I don't remember it.

She stood in the middle of this room, naked, painted gold, pretending to be a statue. Misty vomited in a pot plant and the smell made Melinda sympathy-vomit, revealing that she was actually not a statue, and then she made everyone leave. How could you not remember that, Adelaide?

That's the pot plant I vomited in.

Misty points. Her nail is longer than her finger.

Of course I remember it. I am choosing to no longer acknowledge Melinda's existence and would appreciate your cooperation.

Adelaide pours herself a cup of tea. The amount of steam emanating from the teacup is alarming. She drains the cup in a single gulp and stares down the barrel of the camera.

CUT.

Adelaide has broken the fourth wall. Breaking the fourth wall is a cardinal sin, unless the producers have chosen you to be the season's protagonist. Adelaide has consistently brought some of the show's best stories for four consecutive seasons and has still not been given the starring role. It isn't unreasonable for her to assume that her time has come, this season. But it hasn't and she is wrong. That role belongs to someone else.

Greta has somehow procured a pair of chopsticks and is attempting to nest them amongst her tight curls (she's had a perm) as the camera starts to roll again.

Misty, I think I might need some of your packing tape.

Packing tape? Sorry, doll, I'm not sure what you mean.

Right.

Greta produces a handful of cooked rice from somewhere within the mass of linen that she is swimming in and rolls a few pieces between her fingers. She adds a few more pieces and works the rice into a gum, which she eventually uses to affix the chopsticks to her scalp. Adelaide is disgusted. Misty's eyes have been closed this whole time. A waiter enters the room.

Ladies, the remaining member of your party has arrived.

The remaining member of our party? You dick-breathed morons told me that Melinda's contract had been terminated. If she sets foot in this tea house, I will tear her larynx out with my teeth—

Adelaide, you cannot talk about production matters on camera. We don't have time to cut. Keep rolling. Camera B on the doorway. Enter Jocelyn.

$

As a child, the sound of a pair of stilettos mincing down a corridor roused a particularly potent cocktail of affections within me. Jealousy was the most immediate. A longing to be the subject of that announcement of strident femininity that precedes a billow of jasmine and sandalwood: A woman is entering this room now. There was awe and adoration. Frustration and hope. And of course there was fear. Fear that my cadenced hips and effete wrists would betray the secret all who met me knew, but never thought to name. Flouncing into Madam Takahashi's Eastern Tea House, all I feel is doubt. The culmination of decades of inquisition, therapy and awkward cross-dressing is this, my casting on what *Vulture* ranked the 'Most Misogynistic Television Show of All Time'? It would seem so. And now I am wearing the stilettos, entering a room where three other women are sipping their own cocktails of jealousy and fear. Well, two are. Misty's just sucking hers straight out of the spout of the teapot.

I fought to be a woman. Now, I just want to fight women.

Jocelyn. My hair sits just below my bare shoulders. My neckline is shaven, but you can't see that. A little reminder of the patience it took to watch it grow out. Production asked me if I would consider not shaving for a few days prior to the shoot. It would seem that 'electrolysis' is yet to enter the lexicon of cis cameramen and lighting les-bros. I did offer to glue a fistful of my pubic hair to my neck, but they declined. We ended up having to shoot the promo in a different studio because they hadn't anticipated the possibility of a woman being taller than five foot eight (or six foot two in heels). I was worried that I would look monstrous on camera, but my lack of accidental offspring meant that I was alone on screen and there were no context clues to indicate that I am, in fact, a behemoth. Thank you, science. Production chose my dress. It's fuchsia. It clings tightly to my figure, revealing the indentations between my hips and my waist. The hem hangs two gawking inches above my ankles. My sandals sit upon very small cork wedges. The director of photography actually suggested that I go barefoot before we decided to move to the new studio. Greta must never know about this. As I do a silly little twirl, my back comes into view. All of my tattoos have been covered with foundation. The woman on the screen isn't so much me, but rather a conglomeration of everyone's expectations but my own. She smiles a perfect smile (oral hygiene is genderless). The music fades out; a rabidly plucked harp and the jingling of boat keys.

Still at the end we are denied it and handed the crumbs

BIN BEAUTY

a. t. green

My beauty is a thing I cough up at 3 am—and gently place beside the bin. Blood and glitter and hair and mucus coalesce to create monstrosity that sits pretty in the dark. I smile, smile, smile, too wide; teeth hurt, jaws crack. Under the weight of this effort.

Blood and glitter are not the same viscosity—but both scream FUCK OFF smeared over cheekbones; dripping off chins.

My anxiety is a too-stiff back and a face painted beyond all recognition. Its hiding within smiles and polite conversations. Skitters across floorboards. Whispers in the night and leaves the scent of sour milk. There is nothing amiss, but doom is a word that leads my tongue to trip over itself in the rush to stay silent.

My insomnia passes out drunk at 3 am—wakes up at 5 am, stomach churning and full of regret. It dances with strangers five hours earlier and wakes to the cavalcade of silence stomping past eyelids. It takes acid and benzos and valium and calls no-one in the morning. It does the same thing it has done since high school—it's not nostalgia if you never stopped. It coughs out staccato triplicate beats. My insomnia is a midnight feast at any hour—tiptoeing to the kitchen with its shards of light to rummage for half-baked potatoes. All of its ideas are half-baked but seem cooked depending on the hour. 5 am is rife with good ideas, paint it on a wall, put it in the bank kinds of ideas. My insomnia doesn't understand that people wake next to each other and don't talk about it in the morning.

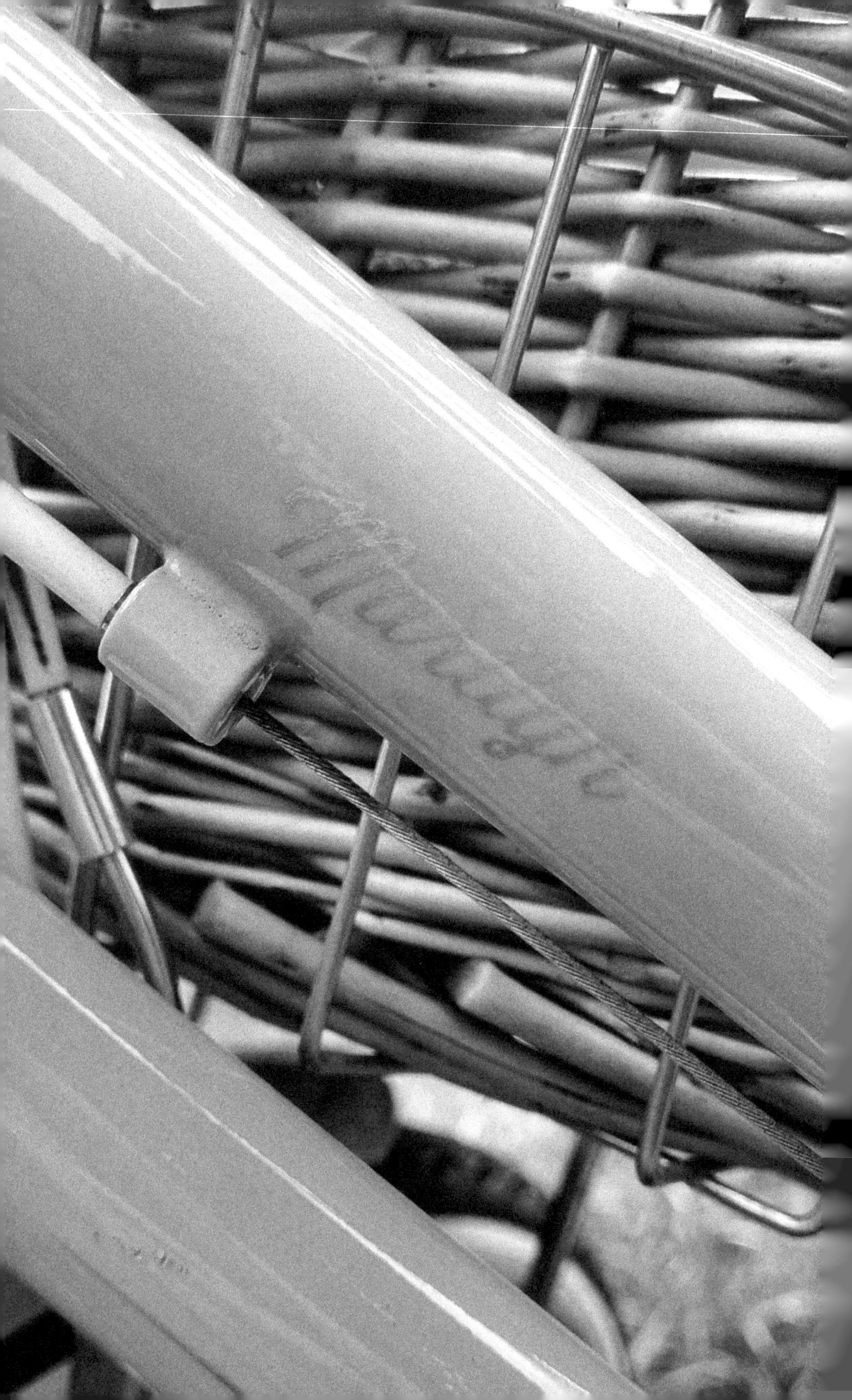

MARILYN

Louis Blake

The room fades in. The weight and position of each of my breasts is not my first thought. Instead, my partner's head lies close against my heart. My chest hair is tickling their nose and I'm already forgetting the dream I was just having. It's fading before my eyes, trailing away from me like fairy floss on the wind, and the harder I try to grab at its ragged ends, the faster they dissolve under my fingers. I resign myself to letting it go. It's something that will never be known unless it wants to be.

I lean down to kiss my partner's forehead, roll over and get out of bed without worrying about my breasts getting caught in some fold or limb or other. I step into fresh pants and consider the forecast I checked last night. It's going to be cool for autumn, but the steady supply of testosterone injected into my glutes means my body runs hotter than it used to, and I know exactly which shirt I want to wear. It's an old one from the women's soccer team I can't play for anymore. Across the front is the team's name in letters so faded only I know what they say anymore: HEART.

I raise my arms to slide the shirt straight over my head and nothing dangles. There is no layer between the shirt and my skin, no layer on top to disguise the shape beneath. I don't need to pretzel my way into two crushing binders that remind me with every breath what they're concealing. I breathe in deep and slow, filling my grateful lungs. My chest expands as far as it can. My body is unburdened. My mind is breathtakingly clear.

I did this all because I had a dream, a different dream to this morning. I died—it was a few years ago; the details are lost to me now—and was immediately rushed to heaven. Something grabbed me by the arms and I was hauled up past the clouds, up towards the moon. It was a dizzying, terrifying height. I saw my body lying dead on the ground becoming a tiny speck as I was whisked away to spend eternity in this form. And I could feel nothing but my breasts weighing heavily on my chest.

I felt that I had been cleaved in two. My eyes snapped open, I rolled over and vomited. I knew something had to change. I could not die like this.

As I leave the house, I don't turn to each side, back and forth, adjusting myself, becoming increasingly frustrated as nothing truly works to make my chest lie flat. I don't avoid mirrors and windows in case they ruin my day. I don't lie in bed for hours, feeling like the weight on my chest is flattening me into the ground. I walk to the shed, get on my bike and ride out into the glorious daylight in just a shirt.

What's left of my tits bounces as I roll over cracks in the pavement. Before, I used to worry that even if I went through with surgery, it would never be enough; the slightest jiggle would remind me of what used to be there. Five thousand grams of flesh, tissue, ducts and lobules, all perfectly functional; I slept a dreamless, chemical sleep and woke up free of them. I used to worry about so many things that don't cross my mind anymore.

My bike is pretty. It's powder blue, upright with swept-back handles and a wicker basket on the front. 'Marilyn' is inscribed in flowery lettering on the frame. It is comfortable and practical and yet it may be the least masculine thing I own. But I don't need to make myself uncomfortable to compensate for discomfort in my masculinity anymore. My masculinity is not so fragile that a powder blue women's bike with a wicker basket can shatter it. My masculinity is so irrepressible I heard it calling through years of repression, suppression, toxicity, denial and discouragement. A call so urgent it finally grew impatient and tore the lid off my dream to shout directly into my brain. So what if people think I'm queer for riding a powder blue women's bike with a wicker basket? I am queer. And I am a man.

I feel a tug when I'm on the bike. When I get home there's a nagging pull inside me that tells me to put away the groceries and come back out, to keep riding. The dam has broken and life is coursing freely through me. I just want to ride and ride all day, even if my legs are screaming. I want to go as far as I can go. I want to never take this freedom for granted.

Air is rushing through my nose, blood through my veins. My leg hair comes to life in the breeze. My shirt whips in the wind as I pedal faster and faster, the faded HEART fluttering across my bouncing man boobs. I'm feeling every input from every cell of my body singing in a thunderous chorus. I am on my bike and it's a beautiful day. I'm grinning the widest grin I ever have.

I ride until the moon comes out and my lights go out, forcing me home. The accumulated insults of the day do not hang heavy on me. I feel tired but light as I step off the bike.

I take off the HEART and nothing dangles. I shower without having to be conscious of every reflective surface in the bathroom. Instead I stand naked in the centre, exposed from all angles. I pose and flex, bouncing each pec in turn, deliberately jiggling the overlying fat, taking in my new body in awe. I show my partner, who laughs and then chastises me for jeopardising my stitches. But there's no pain. I'm healed.

I slide gratefully into bed, not thinking for a second about the placement of my breasts. As my partner puts their ear to my heart again, the dream from this morning comes back to me.

The moon is close. It hangs low in the sky, enormous and heavy, as if the slightest breath of wind would knock it down to shatter on the mountains below. It's irresistible. My feet leave the ground and I fall towards it. I'm not afraid.

It's cool but not cold, a breeze in my hair. The journey of many miles is over quickly, but I fall softly from the moon's sky. The sea of tranquility awaits me. When I enter the water I don't make a splash. I'm instantly enveloped by the warm sea and all the suffering osmoses out of my body. I look back at the earth above me, as I lie beneath the sea, and close my eyes. I don't even need to breathe.

HOME

Nick Lawson

Home is not a place of physicality.

It's the feeling of belonging, emotions sparked from a scent, a memory of having inhaled the alluring aroma of the jasmine-infused skin of someone we once knew and loved.

The intoxicating feeling of safety, of childlike wonder, of all-seeing eyes like a sentry on shift making sure it is only the sun and the moon that arrive as invited and not an asteroid ready to destroy it all.

Do we cease to exist if we are not seen? If we are not heard?
Are we nothing more than what is seen on the outside?

We exist outside of our physical forms and reside between the lines ruled out for us.

Each time you read our words, we exist within you, within these pages, and you feel our presence in the world in which you reside.

We are immortal beings living forever outside the narrative carefully constructed for us by mere mortals.

We speak to you in a way only you can understand.
We make you feel, we make you see, and you hear us and our stories.

You hear our whispers floating in the wind.
Does the wind cease to exist when mortals create beasts to obstruct the path?

Just like the wind, love exists. We know it does; we can feel it.
It connects us with you, each other and the world external to ourselves.

As much as we wish to stay with loved ones, we know that it's not where we belong.
They beg us to stay as the person we are told we are, but it is unbearable to continue to be a lie. A carefully constructed lie in exchange for conditional love and care offered by the world of mortals.

It isn't always as easy as we'd like; we bend to whims and make deviations.
As we carry on our way we find what is looking for us when the time is right.
We find others to share our epic adventure with.
We sing, we dance, and eventually we regrow into ourselves all unbeknownst to many a mortal being.

Even long after we are gone, we will carry on just as the wind, but let us not carry the weight of the world.

'Home' was inspired by the work of Sadie St James,
during the editing of this book.

COTTON

Nick Lawson

COTTON

It was that time of the month for my love
Ther cotton underwear was......
interesting - I can ~~see~~ not look at
them without thinking of my pre
transition days.
~~My~~ ~~ever~~ ex wife thought I was having an
affair after finding my sexy underware
When I hosted ~~the~~ ~~tea~~ a church
bbq. I never even denied it - God
would forgive that sin. God would
want us to stay together. He was not
going to be as forgiving for the troth
I promised not to do it again. So I
bought cotton breifs ~~Underware~~ instead not quite
as nice but soft and sensual against my skin

It wasn't a lie as such more of a half truth. A marriage is built on trust but the only person I was betraying was myself. Demanding to know who the sexy underware belonged to I had to give myself up. ~~I~~ felt like the safest way to reveal myself without ~~her~~ being any real danger to me or me. the chance she'll cotton on to

Who is she!? The woman who wears the red lacy gstring?!

who indeed!!! Oh gosh, what have I gotten myself into? Apart from cotton briefs!? I can't abandon myself again I can't

Pomedoro

In unlikely places we find ourselves

THE COUNTRY IN ME

Adrik Kemp

This piece is based on a series of conversations I had with a close friend of many years about his experiences as a trans person in Australia. It is told in his voice.

I'm from round the traps, in that transient way so many trans people end up being. Bouncing between Melbourne and Sydney by way of Katherine and Yirrkala in the Northern Territory. Depending on when—and where—you meet me, you would know a different side of me unique to that location.

It's tough to pick a shining example of trans experiential excellence, one that is universal but unique, from my own memories, because so often they were more than they appeared.

Take Katherine, for example; it's the best place I ever lived. It has such depth and history in the land and people, something hard to come by anywhere else. As a place, it is a convergence point for three traditional Aboriginal lands, of the Jawoyn, Dagoman, and Wardaman peoples. And the colonial inhabitants are as long-lived on the land as their colonial roots allow them to be. The very earth itself is heavy with history and gravitas.

But I lived in a mundane house in town, and taught kids. I'm a teacher, and this was my first role after starting my transition. It was remarkably easy to get the job, just a phone interview and bob's your uncle, I was on my way to Katherine. But the ease of getting it and keeping it were very different things.

When you've just gone through transition and you get employed as a man, your mind tends to pull you around in circles. Will they want someone who can grow facial hair? Will they wonder why I'm so short? Why my hands are so small? Why my mannerisms, learned from a lifetime of being AFAB, seem so feminine? And why I never, under any circumstances, remove my long-sleeved, button-down shirt?

And all of these thoughts rushed through my head when I first met my boss, who let me know very casually that I had a 'tranny class'.

My mind reeled, already tangled in thousands of strands of self-doubt, 'What?' I thought, 'Is someone taking the piss out of me? Should I be concerned about hidden cameras? What the hell does she mean, a tranny class?'

After some very uncomfortable silence and attempted nonchalance in questioning this, it came to light that in the Northern Territory, they did not refer to this level of schooling as kindergarten or prep. No, it was a transition class. Therefore the children were 'trannies'.

I went to Katherine, and later to the Aboriginal community of Yirrkala, as a way to start my life living openly as a man. It was from Katherine that I flew back and forth to have top surgery. Here was where I continued my transition YouTube channel. And it was in Katherine that I found, in myself, the man I could finally be, comfortable in my own skin.

I was born into a big, typical Lebanese family. And that meant everyone was always up in each other's business. Aunts and uncles feuded and cousins and siblings were underfoot at every turn. And overseeing it all, grandparents and great-grandparents, ensuring our culture remained respected and adhered to by their young Australian progeny. It was loud, warm and close-knit. Unless you were different. And for them, with strong Catholic leanings and a family tradition of preserving our Arab heritage, different was me, personified. I was 'tomboyish' at first and that grew, as it does for many trans men, into presenting as a lesbian who would sporadically date boys to try and save face. And from that into confirming the man I had always been.

When I made the decision and the announcement around my transition, my father stopped speaking to me for two years. Some of my extended family still refuse to even acknowledge me, let alone speak to me, but most of them do. I continue—even after working so hard to be comfortable in my own body, in society—to exist in this state of limbo with my family. I am allowed, to this day, to visit my grandparents, who I love dearly and totally, with every part of me. But when I do, I am forced to use my deadname.

I am asked to remove my facial hair and 'act like a girl' and I comply as best I can. And as the years have passed, this becomes more and more farcical to an outside eye. But it is the price I pay to see my grandparents, relics of another time and unwilling to learn or accept what they see as an unfortunate side effect of modern life.

But in Katherine I was far from this dysfunction, fresh on my transition journey and ready to become the man I knew I could be. There were two ways that I accomplished this, over the years that I lived and worked in the heart of Australia.

The first was by documenting my experiences on YouTube. I had been nurtured over the internet by other trans men sharing their journeys in video diaries. I became friends with and eventually emulated them on my own. I talked about the trials and the setbacks but also the joy of the experience. There is a catharsis in making your transition, a fulfilment of a lifetime of subconscious and conscious desire. So I spoke to my audience.

I talked about my experience searching for a job as a man and the anxiety and thrill of it coming to fruition. I talked openly about the difficulty of obtaining testosterone, vital to my ongoing transition. In my case, there was no doctor in Katherine who could prescribe it for me, so I had to consult my Melbourne-based physician over the phone, and they would then post the script to me for me to take to a chemist. A lot of bureaucratic paperwork for such a simple necessity.

And I vlogged about getting top surgery, flying out of Katherine and back in to get it. When I think back on it, I remember being very careful not to lie about why I had been in hospital. I didn't want to pretend to be sick, so I told people I was 'having some tissue removed', which was technically correct and explained not only the hospital visit, but also the scars. It was only after Katherine, many tattoos and time that I became comfortable and confident enough to go shirtless on a beach, with other men.

I believed then and still believe now that the psychological transition is the most difficult one. Not in seeing myself as a man, which is inherent to who I am, but in understanding that others also see me as a man. When you're raised to cover your chest at all times and then suddenly have an excuse, an *imperative* even, to uncover your chest, it can be mentally very jarring. There are people for whom this isn't the case, of course, but for me, it has been a considered journey.

After a few months in Katherine, my class, in fact the whole school, put on a presentation evening. Children received literacy and merit awards and classes put on performances they had worked on together with their teachers. My class did a resounding rendition of 'Roar' by Katy Perry. It brought the house down. Some might say it was a roaring success.

Once all the kids had been picked up and the teachers remained, we decided to celebrate by going to the best place to go after a school presentation evening in Katherine, and found ourselves at the local Katherine McDonalds.

As I ordered, under the sticky yellow fluorescent light, the young girl behind the counter looked at me sideways and asked, 'Is your name Jack?'.

With a little surprise, I told her it was and asked her if I knew her.

'I love your videos,' she said.

My heart stopped in my chest. I nodded her away from the counter and asked to speak to her more privately. I had to very quickly explain to this young trans girl that I was not out to my colleagues and ask her not to talk about my videos with them. I let her know that I would love to chat more at another time, however, and gave her my number. She was the first of several trans people in the Northern Territory I helped support through various stages of their own transitions.

Even far from my biological family, away from my friends and the cities I'd grown in and lived in all my life, I still found community.

It was early on in my time there that I hatched a plan with a male colleague to kayak down the river. Not something I would do now, with more time and wisdom under my belt, but a great idea then. As we embarked on our ill-advised journey (don't worry, we survived), my friend looked at me sideways and remarked, 'You're very flamboyant, aren't you?'.

Once more, I found myself frozen in place. No doubt I had been talking shit the entire time, oblivious to the possibility of being perceived as a flamboyant man. I had not had my top surgery yet, so was sweltering in 40 degrees in a long-sleeved shirt plus my binder, about to kayak down a river with no shade as far as the eye could see, so perhaps it was my pent-up anxiety doing the flamboyant talking. Or maybe it was just me.

'Am I?' I asked, trying to not clutch my pearls and deepen my voice at the same time. All the while, waiting for a reply, scenarios flew through my mind. As much as I adore it, Katherine isn't the type of place you want to be suddenly outed as any letter of the LGBTQ+ community. In rural Australian one-pub towns, where rodeos are commonplace, men and women work the land and cities are seen as places of great vice and little virtue; being different is frowned upon. And surprising someone with difference is even worse.

I have often wondered about the horrific legality of the 'gay panic' defence laws that until recently existed in various parts of Australia. They run something along the lines of 'I should be exonerated of this crime'—usually bashing or murder—'because I didn't realise the man was gay and when I did, I freaked out, lashed out and now he's dead. But it's really probably his fault, right?' I don't want to start preaching about toxic masculinity and the failing of society on every level in this regard, but that is the root of the fear of being discovered. Beneath the usual worries of ostracism, job loss, reputation loss, there is the underlying threat of violence.

I should say at this point that my friend gave me no indication whatsoever of being a violent person, nor of being an intolerant person. For all I know, he was trying to get me to open up to him because he wanted me to know that I was in a safe space. But I'll never know, because we laughed it off and went on our idiotic kayaking trip together and lived to continue to laugh about it later.

Over time, you pick up mannerisms and build your lexicon from the company you keep and the places in which you keep it. I went to Katherine a 'flamboyant' Sydneysider turned Melburnian, but I left it with irrevocable marks on my personality that remain to this day. I learned to listen to the way the locals spoke, with a casual drawl and a love of laconic Australian slang, the type you read in slang dictionaries from the 1980s but rarely hear in the CBD of any major Australian city. I peppered my speech with them and they became a part of my identity. As I grew into myself as a man, Katherine, and everything it represented, grew into me.

Away from the euphoria of early transition, the events that mark so many trans experiences—the first testosterone injection, top surgery, official changes of name and so on—and into the comparable ease of everyday life as a man, these light-bulb moments of development and change are harder to pin down. But they continue to happen.

I made a choice to live life as a man, not a trans man. And with that choice comes continued secrecy and confusion. Coming out remains something I do regularly, but not in the way of, say, a lesbian or gay person, who might weigh up every new acquaintance and slip in something to indicate their preference simply to make it less awkward. No, for me, it's to friends with years of history, and it causes inevitable change and, more often than not, damage to that friendship. I am married to a woman and we now have kids, so to the average person, we appear to be part of the heteronorm. In this way, I am alienated from the LGBTQ+ community.

The binary joy of early transition has given way to a muddy river of subterfuge and confusion, but within this are islands of safety, my family, my close friendships and my life living outwardly as the person I've always been inside. These are worth more to me than any momentary sadness the river might throw up. They are my reasons for going on.

THE STANDARD YOU WALK PAST

Bron 'Richo' Richardson

On 28 January 2014 I enlisted in the Australian Army. Back then I thought I was going to greatly improve my future, boost my confidence and self-esteem and be a part of a strong and capable team. If I'm honest, I thought the uniforms were pretty cool and there was something appealing about the discipline the ADF presented. I always wanted to be in the Army as a child. I thought camouflage was awesome, and I became fascinated by big military machines after climbing all over a tank at a recruiting display once. I was in the Scouts and enjoyed crawling through the mud when we'd run obstacle courses. Whenever I visited my uncle I'd play dress-ups with his old slouch hat; sometimes he'd indulge me and we'd go on secret missions around the house.

I was adamant that I was going to join the Army when I grew up. I was attracted to the idea of rising to the challenge, doing a tough job and helping my mates out. It seemed masculine and rugged. I pictured myself driving truckloads of food and medicines to remote communities through difficult terrain or helping rebuild after floods or bushfires. It was never about patriotism or going into combat. I just wished to humbly serve those who needed it, lend a hand for little to no reward. I viewed the Army as a noble profession.

When I signed the enlistment form I ticked the 'female' gender option. At the time I didn't think too much about it. At least it would match all my other documents. A few hours later I stepped off the bus at 1st Recruit Training Battalion, Blamey Barracks, Kapooka, not far from Wagga Wagga, New South Wales. My head was freshly buzzed at number 2. I knew the male recruits would have to have their heads shaved that day; it was in our recruitment briefing. I didn't want to miss out on this Army ritual, but I also didn't want to make a scene in case they were weird about women having 'male' haircuts. So on my last day of freedom before enlistment I went to my local barber and got it shaved. I had short hair anyway, so it wasn't exactly a huge difference. At least now I was just like the other men, and nobody could force me to have a long hairstyle. Turns out I needn't have worried. If I wanted my head shaved I'd simply have to volunteer and get it done. They were more concerned about hair being too long and wildly than policing short hair. I got my head shaved again twice during initial training. We lined up like sheep getting sheared and were shorn in quite the same way. Each haircut took about 30 seconds.

Recruit training was much like you see in the movies. As we stepped off the bus we were marched into a darkened building to be sorted into our platoons. Our corporals stood behind camouflage netting, showing only their silhouettes as our names were called out. It was an attempt to intimidate us and began the series of somewhat coercive control techniques used to turn us into soldiers. Over the next 12 weeks we were indoctrinated. There was daily shouting, physical training, lectures, drill, endless cleaning and polishing as well as inevitable punishments whenever we did something wrong. (They always found something wrong.) We dressed the same, spoke the same and marched in time. We ate when they told us. We slept when they told us.

One afternoon a few weeks later, we were marching back to our sleeping quarters, or lines. The corporal in charge complained about our marching form, yelling at us to 'Keep your faggy limp wrists straight while you're f*cking marching'. There were many times this particular corporal had called us 'gay', 'fags' or 'sissies' for doing something incorrectly. On this particular day I felt strong and spoke up once we returned to the lines. I marched up to the corporal's office, where he and the other corporals worked when they weren't yelling at us. I knocked on the door. I was shaking and my voice trembled, but I managed to say that I didn't see how being gay made you any less of a soldier and I didn't think that kind of language should be used. They apologised but said that was just how people spoke and wasn't intended to be homophobic;

however they'd all try to be mindful of their words from now on. I got the sense that they thought I was weak for being offended. Their words said one thing, their attitudes another. Months later, well after the recruit graduation ceremony, one of my old platoon mates came up to me to thank me for my courage. He said I was very brave and, though he was too fearful to come out at the time, found some strength in my actions. Unbeknownst to me, he'd also experienced slurs directed to him personally, both homophobic and racist.

A few days after I spoke out, we had a navigation lecture given by our platoon lieutenant. He made some off-the-cuff comment about civilian orienteering being gay. I tried not to react, keeping my facial expression blank and eyes looking forward. Nobody else seemed to notice. Once we were dismissed he called out my name. 'Recruit Richardson,' he said sternly. 'Sir!,' I barked back, and quickly stood to attention as was required when anybody with his rank addressed us.

I just wanted to get the hell out of there. Why had he singled me out in particular? He apologised for his comments and said he didn't mean to offend me. 'Oh,' I thought, 'That's why me.' At this point I didn't really care about his words or intentions. I just wanted to be invisible. I wish I'd felt stronger at that moment. I wish I'd had the gall and the language to tell him that his words were tokenistic. He wasn't showing integrity or accountability; if he wanted to do that then he should address the rest of the platoon. But I didn't have the strength or the words in me, not this day. 'No worries, sir,' I said. 'It's just how people speak in the Army and you didn't mean anything by it,'—repeating what the corporals had said to me earlier. Back-pedalling my way out. He was satisfied with my response, and I was free to go. I was ashamed for not speaking up but at the same time so relieved the conversation was ended.

I completed my basic training and was posted to Darwin, where I spent the remainder of my four years in the Army. In the beginning I genuinely loved my job—driving the big trucks around and going out bush, getting covered in dirt and becoming completely camouflaged with my surroundings. Tactical driving was fun, and playing with night vision goggles and all kinds of gadgets made me feel like some kind of action hero. I enjoyed the banter with my platoon mates, whether we were in good spirits or suffering through some arduous task at stupid o'clock on no sleep. I enjoyed the physical challenges and exercise, learning that my body was more capable than I gave it credit for, and I grew stronger.

However, the morale at my unit was overall quite low. It slowly infected me. There was this underlying toxic attitude where unless you were a man in a combat role who had been deployed then you were never going to be good enough. At least that's how it seemed to me. Just like in training, there were regular derogatory, off-the-cuff comments and casual taunting. It was considered 'political correctness gone mad' to try and change the culture. The general opinion was that if you didn't like it, you had to toughen up. If you couldn't, you were weak, and if you were ever discovered to be seeing the psychologists on base there was significant stigma attached. Gossip would flare and rumours would spread that you were unfit for duty. I felt out of my depth and alone. I wasn't the only one. In those four years at my unit three soldiers died by suicide, and none of them had ever seen combat.

I did my best to ignore the bad culture. Some days I felt strong and spoke out, though these moments were few and far between. If I spoke out about some derogatory comment or behaviour, I found it hard to explain why I thought it was wrong, just that it was. My vocabulary had been indoctrinated; I could only speak like a soldier. I used Army slang and terminology after work. I became quicker with banter and joking around but struggled in meaningful conversations. I struggled to let the inside out. I was out of practice. I could never find the right language to explain what I felt; no words seemed to fit. I struggled to back up my arguments or to even just have a conversation about my thoughts and feelings. I was scared I would end up looking like a bigger idiot and leave myself vulnerable to taunts. My survival instincts were to keep my head down, go unnoticed and try not to make myself a target. Toughen up and get on with it—or at least pretend to. Surviving meant focusing all my energy on just getting through the day.

With all my energy used up from just surviving, my feelings about my gender identity were getting harder to ignore. I'd never realised just how much I was suppressing my feelings until I found myself in a place where I couldn't express myself at all. Perhaps it wasn't just the toxic environment I was in that brought it to the surface. Perhaps the Army, with its binary and non-binary standards, helped bring it up too. On one hand you could be genderless in the Army. The daily camouflage uniforms were unisex. If you were enlisted, you were referred to by your rank and last name. As long as you could do your job your gender didn't matter; duties were genderless, after all. Perhaps this is why it took me so long to realise. I was quite happy living my best genderless life in many regards. On the other hand gender did matter in some instances. Fitness standards were different for men and women, and there were differences in grooming standards and dress uniforms. It slowly dawned on me that the only time I was uncomfortable about gender was when I was forced to adhere to a 'female' standard. Nobody else was as enraged as I was when they had to follow a standard specific to their gender assigned at birth. I'd joined the most masculine profession I could think of, and yet it wasn't enough for me. I started to ask myself, 'Am I trans?'.

I frantically googled and read all I could, searching for answers. I made friends with trans people outside of the Army living in Darwin. I was horrified but not entirely surprised to learn that they'd had bad experiences with Army members. One friend even admitted to receiving a death threat from one of the members in my battalion. The more I learned, the more I realised that I was already trans and always would be, regardless of whether or not I admitted it to the world. After all of the poor culture I'd experienced, my friend's death threat, the low morale and the alarming number of suicides, I decided that it would be safest to keep my new discovery on the down low. I didn't want to be noticed or singled out as being different. I didn't want to become a target and receive violence or death threats of my own. I knew I needed some help though, so I tried to access counselling through the Army. I knew the counsellors were obliged to confidentiality and as long as I kept my mouth shut outside of those sessions, my unit would never find out. So I made my first appointment, then proceeded to bounce around their system. Nobody seemed to want to help or know how. One doctor even told me not to transition because I would regret it. In the midst of all the chaos

I got a phone call from my parents. My dad had been diagnosed with cancer.

After a few months of turmoil trying to hide myself, without support and on top of carrying the weight of helplessness I felt about not being able to help Dad, I decided to just leave. It took me a few months to finalise all the paperwork and jump through all the hoops to actually discharge, but I did it. By January 2018 I was back home in Melbourne. I'd walked away from a career, but I'd also saved myself from a toxic workplace that was costing lives one way or another. Over the next two years I allowed myself to explore my identity free from the military's standards and restrictive culture. I was embraced and celebrated by my friends and family, by the LGBTIQA+ community. I was gently held as I found my words and learned how to express myself, free of shame and guilt. I was encouraged to speak, even if my words weren't up to date. A good friend told me, 'You can learn the politically correct language later; it's more important to get the words out first. It ain't healthy to be emotionally constipated.' I slowly began to find my voice, finally putting words to some of my thoughts and feelings. I began to change my language from soldier to civilian. I found strength in the diversity of expression in the safe spaces of the LGBTIQA+ community. When Dad died I was held and allowed to grieve. I wasn't encouraged to toughen up and get on with it like I would have been in the Army. Whatever ugly mess I needed to be, I could be. No judgement or shame.

Meanwhile the #MeToo movement gathered momentum, and there were many conversations happening around me. Listening to these helped me find my language and put words to some of the experiences I'd had in the Army. I now understood how misogyny influenced the Army culture. I could articulate it now. As the global pandemic hit, I spent more time on social media to fill the void of lockdown and boredom, reading articles and comments and learning about statistics, case studies and new terminology. By May 2020 the Black Lives Matter protests had erupted all over the world. The conversations expanded to talk about how Indigenous

Australians are both convicted of crimes and imprisoned at a disproportionately high rate. I first heard the term ACAB (All Cops Are Bastards), and with the shooting of Kumanjayi Walker by former soldier, now cop, Zach Rolfe, along with the release of the Brereton Report, I began to see 'F*ck the cops' and 'F*ck the troops' in the same posts.

Now, I'm the first to admit that the Army can be problematic in many ways. You don't have to look far to find scandalous reports of sexual assault, hazing, abuse of power, bullying and misogyny within the Australian Defence Forces. The Brereton Report has uncovered war crimes committed by Australian Special Forces in Afghanistan. One of the recipients of Australia's highest award for bravery, the Victoria Cross, Ben Roberts-Smith, is alleged to have committed unlawful killings, bullying and domestic violence. It is also true that numerous far-right extremist groups boast ex-ADF personnel amongst their ranks.

Even when I joined in 2014, the Army was recovering from a sexual abuse scandal and had come down hard on the offenders. The then Chief of Army, Lieutenant General David Morrison, gave his famous speech, saying, 'I will be ruthless in ridding the army of people who cannot live up to its values… The standard you walk past is the standard you accept.'

I have to admit I was inspired by his speech. I believed that the Army was trying to purge itself of the toxins of poor culture and misogyny, and I wanted to help. I still believe the Army is trying to change, but to achieve such a change will take a long time. Much longer, as it turned out, than I was willing to wait.

Witnessing my friends shout anti cop/soldier sentiment and smearing hate online made me withdraw into my shell. I was conflicted. I did not (and still don't) doubt for one second that systemic racism exists within the police, other government agencies and indeed within society as a whole. I also agreed (and still do) that policing, defence and government help perpetuate colonialism and uphold problematic systems of oppression. I was still very angry at the Army, but I believed that it could do some good. 'Having a group of trained personnel with large-scale logistics capability can be very useful,' I thought. Can we still have these institutions helping serve our society without all the unjust and unnecessary racism, sexism, homophobia, transphobia and xenophobia? Can we just get the police to catch rapists and paedophiles instead? Can the ADF just be a peacekeeping force and help out in emergencies?

I knew it was more complicated than that, but there was just no space for diversity of thought on the subject. The peer pressure to uphold the norms of the social media echo chamber was crippling. I'd seen people attacked, 'cancelled' and ostracised for having any alternative opinions. 'Does anyone know my work history?' I thought. 'Would they be just as violent toward me if they knew?' I catastrophised and spiralled downwards. The very same community that had held me so gently as I needed to heal and find myself would seemingly turn their back on me now if they knew I had been in the Army, or if I had any differing opinions on the police or the ADF.

Here I was, a now-cis-passing white man, and ex-Army at that, existing in this world where men who looked like me were the enemy. As a descendant of white immigrants living on stolen land, I knew I benefited from the ongoing effects of colonialism. I became paralysed not only with white shame and guilt but also with the shame of my past and my complicated feelings about the Army. I found it hard to move forward. I watched on as others tore the police and the ADF to shreds in online posts, on signs and yelling at rallies. I tried to do all the things I thought were right—donated to worthy causes, shared online posts and tried to educate myself—but speak about my views I did very little. How could I be so angry at the Army from my own experiences, agree with the collective that systemic racism and sexism exist within ADF yet still believe in it somehow? I became overwhelmed with all of the noise, the call-outs, the cancel culture, the vitriol. I wanted to still belong in the community spaces that had held me so tenderly as I grew into myself. People were angry, and rightly so. I was angry too! I just didn't want their anger directed at me because of my past or because I had complicated feelings.

There was lots of noise. I felt conflicted between my past and my present. The person that once wanted to join the Army was still in me. I was still attracted to the idea of belonging to a giant team with equipment that could help people out if they needed it. Was that the problem? Had the Army exploited me by selling me that idea in exchange for four long years of questioning my morals and hard labour? Was I wrong to even enlist in the first place, or was it an honourable sacrifice? While I'd seen women, people of colour and people from other minorities rise through the ranks, I knew it couldn't have been easy for them. The glass ceiling still existed—though maybe with new policies and folks like Lieutenant General Morrison at the helm it was only a matter of time before that changed.

The truth was, I still didn't think being in the Army was entirely good. I didn't think it was entirely bad either. I knew I wouldn't be the person I was without the experience I'd had in the Army. It had become somewhat of a burden on my identity. I struggled to call myself a veteran and be proud, yet I'd so happily say I was proud to be trans. I knew the identities were not mutually exclusive; they just hadn't learnt how to be in the same body as each other yet. It was, after all, hard to be what I couldn't see. I didn't know anyone with similar experiences and similar feelings about the ADF. I knew, though, that it was time to navigate these identities and start opening up about my feelings, or I'd be stuck in this turmoil.

I heard about a rainbow wreath-laying ceremony held on Anzac Day each year. Its aim was to honour the diversity of military service and in particular pay tribute to LGBTIQA+ service personnel. I thought that attending might begin in some way to reconcile my trans identity with my Army past. I caught a train into the city and walked the rest of the way to the Shrine of Remembrance. I wore my service medal and my trans pride pin. I felt like they were both targets on my jacket, but I still felt it important to be visible.

It was a solemn and humbling ceremony. All the noise of my inner conflict didn't seem to matter as a handful of people gathered in the powerful silence of the crypt and laid the wreath. I made friends with some of those who attended and found some strength in solidarity. Over the next few months I learned to open up again and talk about my feelings. I unpacked and questioned my own choices, actions and thinking. I found my humility. Humans are allowed to be complicated and flawed and don't always have to have all the answers. I began to understand that perhaps I would always feel complicated about the Army and that it was okay.

TIMBERWOLF

Isabelle Quilty

I emerge from the womb of the storm with purpose and pale lips. Memories of the storm ripple in my wake, black water rushing past my ankles.

These shores are lonesome, greeted only by timber planks, and torn sails get caught in the teeth of the rock walls. Dawn begins to warm my back, and for this I am grateful.

No others survived the shattering. Like the mist glancing from the ship's bow (once formed) they fell back to the ocean.

So, I stand alone, the sun of my homeland drying the salt and pain of the travels to my back.

> I wonder, breathless
>
> Heedless
>
> Bound with countless warnings
>
> But the gentle lap of the tide reminds me
>
> This will all be worth it in the end.

Upon the crest of a hill sits a wooden temple that watches the rolling hinterlands like a crown upon a king's head. Within, there are countless souls formed of wax and wood. They sit and debate amongst themselves, wondering which god will hear them first. I find an axe buried in a stump, and free it with one swift motion.

The temple awaits me, too.

Within, two idols with pale, cedar eyes watch me. The first is a mother that clutches her swollen belly.

The second is a wolf, his jaws frozen in a fierce snarl. (Despite the axe in my knuckle-white grip I avert my eyes. They are gods, after all.)

I kneel before them and the axe clatters beside me. The candlelight flickers in the reflection of the blade.

> The mother has honey-bee wax pressed into the ripples in the wood, gleaming.

> She watches me
>
> The matriarch
>
> Mother
>
> Protector
>
> Expects me to follow in her footsteps
>
> As the gods wish it
>
> To fit the design.

I lift the axe and as the tongues of flames lick hungrily, I swing, and the pleasuring sound of the crack of wood and worship rings in my ears.

I leave the axe, buried in her navel. Red wax bleeds from my strike, weeping.

The wolf breathes down my neck, a howl on its worn snout.

All that I have done is to honour the god buried in my heart from the moment I was born.

The blade running through my hair.

My fingers, sticky with the honey and flour that I will offer in place of the mother.

The stones that have pressed down my ribs, the grip of a giant's hand around me, insisting I bear the pain for the sake of survival.

The splinters of the mother will always remain within me.

But I am the wolf.

The false idol.

Owed offerings of fire, wax and honey.

In a world that will never give me such things.

THE VAMPIRE IN THE HOUSE

Rowan Heath

I've been thinking about vampires. In *The Vampire: A New History*, Nick Groom argues that vampires have become so embedded in Western culture since the Enlightenment that they're used as symbolic devices to explore basically everything, from life and death, medicine and religion to politics and capitalism. As cultural artefacts, vampires have an amazing ability to apply to almost anything while also being distinct and enigmatic. Reading *The Vampire*, I sometimes felt like I was reading about myself. The vampire's fundamental symbolic qualities apply to a lot of what I know about being transgender. The vampire Groom describes is so applicable to my experience that it feels uncanny.

In hindsight, I've realised that the vampire appeals to me because I struggle to find symbols for transness. When I write about being trans, I'm explaining something I've never had the tools to explain to an audience that doesn't have the tools to understand me. I'm wary of using symbols that weren't developed by people like me, but they're often the only symbols I have. When I talk about gender dysphoria to people who know little about it, I fall back on old analogies even though they're inadequate, because it's the only way I can explain myself while holding my listener's attention. I say, 'Imagine living in someone else's body,' or 'It's like wearing clothes that don't fit right'. But I need to modify these analogies if I want to use them accurately, and if I do that, by the time I've explained myself I no longer have my listener's attention. It's easy to say, 'I was born in the wrong body,' because the idea that a 'masculine' mind can exist in a 'feminine' body slots neatly into how many of us understand sex and gender. But this phrase is flattening. When I use it, I squeeze my experience into a slim, easy-to-digest narrative. It's not useful to me anymore.

Vampires are special because they're amorphous; they can be everywhere and everything. They're in our books, movies, comics and music. You can be playful with vampires; they can be your enemy, your lover, your evil twin, your boss or simply the supernatural plague on your town. Vampirism bleeds into real life.

We conjure vampires through the language of predation, exploitation and bloodsucking.[3] Think of all the professionals you might describe as vampiric: lawyers, stockbrokers, politicians, perhaps even doctors. Think of the words we associate with criminality—what comes to mind? Cold-blooded, predatory, monstrous, deviant?

According to Groom, vampires are a product of society rather than a single person's imagination. They emerged from a clash between science, superstition, politics and law in the 18th century.[4] When we talk about vampires, we draw on more than just coffins, blood and long incisors; we invoke the cultural weight they've accrued from centuries of association with medical, political and religious discourse. Vampires are still around because the questions they presented in the 18th century are relevant today—questions about disease, medicine and how we inhabit our bodies. Vampires disrupt 'everyday life by exposing the shortcomings of the ways in which we make sense of our experience'.[5]

I can use vampirism to understand why my loved ones reacted to my transition the way they did, and to interpret how it felt to come out to a family that hadn't seen transness before yet still had preconceptions about what transness meant. However, I want to note that this conversation is fragile and the reader might easily be misled. Trans people aren't vampires, but our culture colours transness with the language and ideas of vampirism in a way that contextualises my experience.

---

[3] Nick Groom, 2018. *The Vampire: A New History* (New Haven: Yale University Press), 43.

[4] *The Vampire*, 24.

[5] *The Vampire*, 160.

Vampires are inescapably corporeal

The complexity of the undead body is an important feature of vampirism. The vampiric body—by day, an incorruptible, lifelike corpse; by night, a mobile horror engorged with the lifeblood of others—threatens the integrity of the living body through its insatiable bloodlust and immunity to decay. The vampire is not quite living, not quite dead; it's recognisably human, yet inhuman enough to be an entirely different creature. By challenging what it means to be alive, the vampire also challenges what it means to be human.

When I came out, I was immediately quizzed about my plans for my body. Transition was inescapably corporeal. I'd never had such explicit importance placed on my body before, and the things that I wanted to change—my chest, my shape, my voice—were suddenly treated as sacred. By masculinising my body, I threatened its integrity. My family viewed top surgery as an unnecessary amputation and hormone therapy as dangerous and unnatural. They feared transitioning would disfigure me. Their concerns reveal a lot about what we expect women to be and value. What if I was an ugly man? What if no-one could love me after surgery? What if hormones sterilised me? These questions involved imaginary people—future partners, future children—whose opinions I had to take into account. My body had communal value, and protecting that value was more important than alleviating my discomfort.

I can account for my family's protests while acknowledging that they still cared about me by comparing a certain perception of transness to vampirism. To them, transness might've had the same inhuman, monstrous symbolic weight as vampirism. Both disrupt the ways in which we make sense of human experience. While the vampire challenges what it means to be human, transness challenges what it means to inhabit a body when we are expected to treat it a certain way. By transitioning, I undermined something as unshakable as the line between life and death.

The challenges vampirism and transness pose to normative culture are largely symbolic, and as threats to the norm they share connotations. Trans-affirming health care is glutted with vampiric language, charged from 18th-century discourse that understood vampirism as unnatural, immoral and destructive. Mastectomies aren't transgressive or immoral unless they're performed on trans people; the treatments used for precocious puberty aren't invasive, destructive or unnecessary until given to young trans people. While the procedures and treatments don't change, because they're administered for the purpose of transitioning, they take on the vampiric language of transgression.

Vampires 'create themselves through the destruction of others'[6]

Vampires created through infection are the result of the inherently destructive transformation of a living human into a corpse, and then into an undead being. Identity is the paradox at the heart of the vampire: is the vampire a loved one possessed, or a loved one transformed? What remains of the person who inhabited the body? Transness, in the vampiric sense, is destructive of the cis body in the same complex way. To many, my trans body is a disfigured cis body, and transition destroyed the girlhood that was integral to my identity.

If transition causes the symbolic death of the cis body, then trans people can symbolise the undead. Before transitioning, my body carried a certain set of values and ideals. I undermined these values by unavoidably inscribing transness onto my body, and for my family, this was a transgression against life. By transitioning, I killed essential parts of myself—girlhood, womanhood—yet like the wakeful dead, I was still around.

If my family hadn't placed so much implicit value on cisgenderism, we might've seen my transition solely as growth, or simply another change. But like the transformation of the vampire—which necessitates death—my transition was associated with loss, and so my family grieved. I'll never shake that feeling. The vampire tells me that they grieved because our culture taught us that transition would destroy me. I can't help but relate this perception of 'undeath' with the contradiction of life in an identity (and body) that was dead to me.

Transitioning hasn't killed me. Rather, I've gained so much. This self-knowledge has given me context for my lifelong

---

6 *The Vampire*, 129.

discomfort and the information and care I needed to inhabit my body comfortably. Before I knew I was trans, I was going to spend my life rotting away at home. If I was ever undead, it was before I transitioned. There's irony in the idea that my family began to grieve me only once I came to life.

Vampires are a threat to the community

In some 18th-century accounts, vampires are giant, deadly vermin. They spread disease and death to livestock and people and destroy household and agricultural tools.[7] Newborn vampires targeted their relatives first, starting with their immediate family, then moved on to menace their community.[8] A single vampire could destroy generations of an extended family through killing and infection.[9]

My transition exposed some very rigid values my family upheld (myself included), which made it difficult for us to process the change I needed. My transition was inevitably a family matter because I needed my family's support, but I didn't transition in a cultural vacuum, and these values aren't unique to my family. Transness, like vampirism, is something of a community matter. I receive pamphlets in the mail offering dubious spiritual cures for 'gender troubles'. More medical professionals than I care to remember have refused to treat me properly because I'm trans. Elections increasingly centre people like me and what level of our involvement in society can be tolerated.

Something interesting happens when we apply the vampiric language of predation and disease to transness. The vampire isn't just a threat to a single home; they menace entire communities. The destruction of a loved one by vampire—or worse, the transformation of a loved one into a vampire—isn't a personal tragedy but a communal one. When a single family is targeted by a vampire, the whole community is both in mourning and at risk. Transness has similar weight, as a symbolic disruption of heteronormative culture. Transness is too often addressed in a language that portrays trans people (especially trans women) as

---

7 *The Vampire*, 14.
8 *The Vampire*, 12.
9 *The Vampire*, 35.

social deviants and sexual predators—a narrow, bigoted view that highlights its 'threat'.

Yet unlike vampires, trans people exist, and they're some of the most vulnerable people in our communities because of how they are perceived. From legislation that restricts our life activities to outright violence, trans people suffer the consequences of the perceived threat of transness more than anyone else.

Vampires are an epidemic

Vampirism is contagious. It's spread through infected bites and infected blood. Historical outbreaks of vampirism were both 'a symptom and a cause of an ailing or traumatized body politic.'[10] While some 18th-century sceptics attributed vampires to mass delusion,[11] vampires were addressed by medical discourse, so they became real and part of the history of infectious diseases.[12] Scientific understanding of disease has changed since the Enlightenment, yet the vampire has a contemporary resonance with epidemics. Vampirism is emblematic of pre-Enlightenment contagions, such as the Black Death, once thought to spread through corrupt air and considered by some to be divine punishment for immoral behaviour.[13] Cholera outbreaks in the 19th century found a modern scapegoat in doctors who were already associated with vampirism because they'd spent the previous century dabbling in the strange, occult art of medical science, stealing corpses for dissection and prescribing bloodletting.[14]

Transness is often portrayed as a modern contagion coded with vampire thinking: modern because it supposedly spreads, like a trend, through social contact with trans people; vampiric because it is contagious, predatory and destructive. I can open most newspapers and find rhetoric that argues transness is a dangerous, immoral lifestyle choice, a fad or a mass delusion indulged by otherwise healthy people. I've been asked if I transitioned because

---

[10] *The Vampire*, 44.
[11] *The Vampire*, 76.
[12] *The Vampire*, 15.
[13] *The Vampire*, 16.
[14] *The Vampire*, 165.

of something I saw on the internet, or if I'm buying into a trend. I think of all the politicians, celebrities, authors and academics who treat transness as a public health crisis in the sense that trans people are a threat to public health. My local community is filled with educated, empathetic people who use the vampiric language of contagion, predation and degeneracy when they talk about trans people and 'trans ideology'.

The ultimate predator doesn't just harm directly but proliferates harm by spreading itself across the community. It poses both a physical and a symbolic threat. Like vampires (who were once innocent and human), trans people are both the victims and proponents of an imaginary contagion that plagues the body politic. In the vampiric sense, transness is a destructive condition that starts with an infected individual and bleeds out into the family, the community and eventually the nation to destroy society from within. Whereas vampires in the 18th century symbolised the collapse of secular society and the instability of the human body,[15] trans people are used as working metaphors for the collapse of heteronormative society. As an alternative to normative conceptions of gender, transness threatens the stability of the gender binary that is so integral to Western culture. For many people, trans people are the vampires of the here and now; contagious and predatory, undermining the integrity of the nation.

Vampires are immune to decay

Trans people, of course, aren't vampires. We're humans trying to get on with our lives. One of the hardest parts of coming out was the culture that informed me that my body became sacred when I tried to change it, that I had to have shown obvious signs of being trans in early childhood and that transitioning was akin to death. I wasn't born in the wrong body, but my body did grow in a direction that didn't suit me. When I finally figured that out, my culture was already primed to make it difficult for me to change.

I've created a grim portrait of the present by using the vampire as a symbolic device. However, I'm optimistic—my mum didn't understand how much I needed top surgery until long after

---

[15] *The Vampire*, 91.

I had it, but she still washed my hair for me while I recovered. The important people eventually came round.

I want to finish on something else I know about transition—something that's been hard for me to find anywhere but amongst other trans people, that has taken me years to pin down and that I will probably spend the rest of my life trying to understand. Transition is growth, and for things to grow, usually other things need to decay. Both are natural. If they weren't, fruit wouldn't rot, hair wouldn't grow and there'd be no such thing as compost. Our bodies would freeze where we buried them. Vampires don't decay—that's why we find them unnatural. When I think of my transition and the things I left behind—the name I was born with, the chest I had removed, the hair I cut off—it seems like a simple process of decay and growth. What's so unnatural about that?

HAPPINESS

Hailey McKenzie

Lo-fi beats drift slow and lazy—the squeak of shoes on hardwood mingles with the hiss of steamers. Baristas and customers hum with polite conversation, accented with the ding of EFTPOS machines. Plants adorn every available surface. Sunlight bathes the air in mahogany tones. Under it all is the low rumble of the espresso machine producing the city's lifeblood. While it's not quiet, it's cosy and calm. The kind of calm that nestles inside you, trying to take root.

I sit in a corner booth, drinking my latte. With each sip, the atmosphere soaks in deeper. I can't shake the feeling that I've been here before. This is the ur-cafe, the platonic ideal of a coffee house. As though Melbourne's entire coffee scene was fed through a grinder, and this distilled from the remains.

With each mouthful, the deja vu grows.

'Hey there, everything okay? Anything I can getcha?' The waitress appears suddenly, a picture of denim and flannel. There's an American twang to her—and an ageless quality in her face.

'Ah, no thank you, I'm good,' I stammer out. I've always been nervous with strangers.

'Ya sure? Nuffin' ya want? Soda? 'Nother coffee?' she insists.

'N-no, I'm waiting for someone,' I stammer again.

God, just go already.

'A'ight, but if ya need anything, don't hesitate.'

She's gone before I muster a reply.

A chill begins to seep into my fingers. I fidget with my skirt hem. Between the tights, beanie and Doc Martens, I don't feel cold much.

Then, footsteps. The kind that cut through. They belong to a boy. Fifteen. Hair messy, shirt rumpled. His backpack is tatty, his shoes scuffed and worn. There are dark rings under his eyes.

Too little sleep and too much dread. He drops into the booth across from me and pulls out a novel. I go to say something, but the words die in my mouth.

'HAILEY, MY DARLING!' I wince at the loud proclamation.

Mother.

She's followed the boy in like an overbearing shadow. She cups my face in both hands, dragging my cheeks to meet her lips. She's not who I'm here to see.

'Mum, off.'

'Oh, sorry Bubby, it's not every day I get to see my precious bo—gi—uh…child.' She cycles through genders with distaste.

'Girl, Mum, just say girl.' I sigh. This has always been a sore point.

'Okay, it's not an attack!' She throws her hands up in exasperation.

'Anyway, it's so good to see you, I missed you so much and…' I switch off. I've heard all this before. I nod, smile and placate. Slip-ups about my gender stick in like barbs. The waitress brings her a coffee and nods to me in sympathy. The boy glances at us over his book.

'Well, I should be going. Your gorgeous brothers won't wrangle themselves!'

I mutter a silent prayer of thanks.

'Oh, before I go, I wanted to ask you something.' Her tone lands at the crossroads of ignorance and concern.

'Were you happy?'

'Yes, Mum.' My response comes out guarded and robotic.

'You don't regret this lifestyle choice?'

'No, mum, it's not a—' I take deep breath. 'No, I don't.' Resignation hangs heavy in the answer. It's what I've come to expect.

'Okay, good.' She leans over and kisses my forehead. 'Bye Bub, love you.' As quickly as she stormed in, she's gone.

What follows her is a procession of familiar faces. Perhaps everyone I've ever known. Each makes polite conversation. Each ends with the same question: 'Were you happy?'

Each utterance is frustrating. Each answer more strained. The boy peeks over the book, listening intently. There are only two visitors that break with tradition. The first is a man. He comes quietly. The stink of booze and rot creep off him like cockroaches. He crashes down and opens his mouth. Rage and malice radiate from him.

I throw my coffee in his face.

He melts. The waitress brings me another drink.

The second is a woman in a sundress. It's floral, covered in sunflowers and daffodils. She says nothing, but kisses my cheek, sits, and interlaces our fingers. We have matching rings. As our hands touch, I remember. Our first meeting, our first kiss, our home, our life, and our eventual goodbye.

She leans in to whisper, 'Don't take too long, okay?'.

'Yeah, see you soon, Sausage.' She nods at my response, a cheeky smile on her face. She leaves, gliding; graceful.

'Sure ya don't wanna go after her?' The waitress is standing beside me. I don't know how long she's been there.

'No, waiting on one more.'

'Well, don' wait too long.'

She's gone again.

I look over at the boy. Our eyes meet and I wave him closer.

'Your turn, Kiddo.' He rolls his eyes and gathers his things. He's as slow as black tar on a sloth. Completely counter to the rush of his arrival. He takes a seat. For a moment, it's like looking in a mirror. I see the same insecurities that still cling to me. I see a thirst for love, respect, recognition. I see anger and hatred too. They're brighter than my own, not dulled by time, effort or compassion. He's still a dam ready to burst.

Then he raises the walls, slips into the nihilistic mask we once found comforting, and the recognition is gone. He refuses to look me in the eye.

'So, we're some kind of fairy now?' He doesn't use 'fairy'. He says something much harsher. A word that I spat in my teens, denied pre transition, and shunned post. There was a time I saw red at its use. Would sock the one who said it. But time and love have shown that violence is something to be measured, restrained, and doled out as a last resort.

'Not quite the word I would use.' Disappointment colours my tone.

'Then what is this?' Outrage colours his.

'Being true to ourselves.'

'Nah, I'm not a queer.' Again, not the word he used. I remember his pain.

'Your secret cross-dressing, web history and boyfriends say otherwise.' I play up the campness, just a little. Partially it's to piss him off, and partially it's for my own enjoyment.

'Shut the fuck up.' His words a mumble.

'Make me.' I give a reply I've used since I was nine. He's looking down at the table. Arms crossed. Withdrawn.

'Are we…' His voice is quiet, and there's a little crack, like he's afraid to finish the sentence. 'Are we like this because of him?' He finishes it, and my heart breaks. I forgot how fragile I was back then. A glass cannon, all fire and fury 'til I cracked.

'Oh, Kiddo, no.' I grab his hand and hold it. 'We are this in spite of him. What he did to us growing up was abhorrent. But it doesn't define us. We grew. Thrived. Came into our own despite our trauma, not because of it.'

He sniffles and fights back tears. I let mine flow freely. It's a while before conversation picks up again.

'Were we happy?'

It's such a simple question.

Such a monumental task to answer.

I inhale deeply.

'Yes and no. Happiness is subjective. But we got happier. We met new people, made new friends. We started moving forward, we learned to love ourselves…' For a moment I see flowers. 'Eventually we learned to love others too.'

'Was it hard?'

'Yeah. All good things are.' I take one final sip of my drink before I get up. I dust myself off and throw my backpack over my shoulder. It's tatty. Some things don't change. I offer the kid my hand. 'Come on, it's time to go. She's waiting.' He stands up and we walk hand in hand towards the exit.

The waitress winks as I pass, out into a field of daffodils and sunflowers.

Until we take the steps we will never begin our journey towards making it our reality

UPLANDER

Eliot Jane Walton

Lister is in the temple storeroom—where the gods' grain is housed when times are good. It is a butcher's shop now; the dead lie on tables in various states of decomposition. One table is covered in clay pots smeared with blood, and the other contains notebooks whose pages are wavy with moisture.

She learned to write in the saddle of a horse. Her people are always moving. Many summers ago, her family came from the uplands to trade leatherwork and wool for the grains and trinkets of the Empire's city. Uplander leatherwork is prized—and Lister's the most prized of all. Her family stayed when the caravans left, as have many of the uplanders.

There have always been rumblings about them: how can one live on the edge of a vast country and not wonder about the people who live there—who move and make a home for each season? Once in a generation—so the uplanders tell us—the Empire gathers itself to expand its borders and bring them to heel. Then we see a column of armoured men ride out with their wagons and the banner of Empire snapping in the wind. If they return, they complain of pneumonia, indigestion and malnutrition. The uplanders melt into the distance. The rains, winds and snows do the rest.

I have seen it once already, though I am only young. So, I pay no attention when the soldiers first come, and ignore the soft man—the General—who declares martial law. They will pass like wind in the reeds, say the old women; watch them leave as soon as this summer-sickness is done.

But winter has come and the ground is too hard for burying. The old women are silent as the General declares that the sickness has come from the uplands. He seems sorry to say it, says the quarantine will be short. The soldiers are moved from the barracks and housed in the city.

The uplanders are turned out of their homes. They do not belong, says the General, and they must be moved. They are pushed into the barracks; bewildered, they look around as the normal order of the world is turned upside down. The soldiers build a wall around the uplanders' new quarters. They mark it with a U and forbid anyone to go there.

I hear about this from the children, who hide their faces but will tell you anything for hot soup. I live with the temple women; our faces are thin, and our eyes are hollow. We used to be respected and consulted; the old magistrate never decided without us. But the General has no time for gods—and we are made to know how little we matter to him.

We ought to rise up, I think. We ought to light the streets on fire, to overpower the soldiers and beat them with their own truncheons. We ought to say that we will not tolerate this treatment of the uplanders—I wish we would rise up so they would learn to respect us.

I wish—but no more. So, the uplanders are taken from their homes, and the soldiers burn their belongings, saying they are tainted. I am so close that the heat slaps my face—but I do not rise against it.

I sleep through the morning and rise when the other nurses shake me. They wash, undress and curl up with each other under blankets. I turn my eyes from them and feel the heat in my cheeks.

I wash, and dress in my rags. I take a tray in to Lister, a pot of tea, some stale bread and soup. Her workshop is rank, and even I, who am used to the courtyard of fifth, am disgusted. She sprawls in the middle of her chamber—her bad leg extended before her. The sticks she uses to hold herself upright lie abandoned. Aside from using her chamber-pot, I don't think she moves anymore.

I set her tray down. I press a hand to my chest. I wait. An unsteady hand brushes the bread and breaks off a little. I sigh and she looks at me. Her fire-eyes have dimmed; I see so little of the fierce girl from my youth. Her mother is the temple warden—perhaps this is why she is here and not in the barracks with her people. Perhaps the General thought she could defeat the plague, like a hero of legend who, at a word, can turn back the wind.

I leave and return with a basin of water and a bar of soap. I am determined. Lister lowers her eyes, her cheeks red. She lets me undress her—lets me chafe her feet between my hands and begin to wash them. A ceremony of sorts, the washing of a traveller's feet. She is no traveller, but I wash them all the same.

She lies down as I work, her chest rising and falling. Though I am only doing my duty, I find there is heat in me, heat enough to chase away the cold. I work slowly, taking my time to pray. I feel the muscles of her feet with my fingers, while I slide, smooth and separate them. Her right foot is formed strangely, and without her sticks she cannot walk. If she once fell from the saddle or if she was born this way, I cannot tell.

I move on to her calves, feeling the ridges of her bones and the crust of grime on her skin. I wash and find myself singing the prayers of healing and homecoming. Lister gasps at the press of my hands—then makes small noises, whether of shame or pleasure I cannot tell. Let me do some small part to heal this city. If I cannot save any others, let me at least save her. Let me at least save myself.

I move higher and wash the grime from between her thighs. She sighs and I think for a moment she might have passed away. But her hand finds mine and squeezes. My heart flutters and my fingers tremble.

I move to her hips, her stomach, where the landscape of her body is corrugated by the lines of ribs. I bend to my task and my hair falls. She shivers when it brushes her skin. I imagine her mother pleading with the General—promising Lister would stop the plague and save the sick, if only she could stay in the temple.

I imagine the General leaning closer. I imagine that he has decided: I will let her stay in, let her understand what it is to be human. This she has learned. To be human is to live within a body with animal needs: to be fed and rested and to see the sun. All industry is secondary.

A body can entertain notions of justice and cures only so long as the body is well. It forgets these when it is exhausted, starved and made to live in its own filth. I peel the last of her layers off and sit astride her. Lister's body tenses beneath me—I feel my own respond. She covers herself for modesty—how can she still feel shame? I speak softly, and she puts her arms back. I feel her relax.

I wash her. I do not pray. I do not mind the trembling in my fingers—I do not mind it at all. If she feels it—the heat in me running to her—she does not speak. Only she tilts her head. Closes her eyes. I concentrate, and listen to the sound of our breathing, the running of the water and the cries of the dying, outside this place.

I leave her in a daze. It seems to me that I float past all the other women, that I have in me some new light—some fire—which will never burn out. All things seem inconsequential; I am the red earth now, which watches the seasons but still endures. The earth, I think, is a sleeping woman, who will one day shake off this paltry Empire and crush its little men under the weight of eternity.

I do not know if the others see the change. I sew bodies into sheets and carry them into the back of a wagon which is housed behind the temple. The horses snort in their stables and whinny. I do not know why we are both healers and carrion carriers. The bodies are stacked like firewood. Some are stiff with the cold and others with death itself. I think of Lister and the heat moves through me.

I sleep in the afternoon and will be woken during the darkest hours to take the bodies away. The General will not have it seen that death takes the uplanders too. He will prosecute his war on these people, and some future historian may think him worth a single line of print. That is all we shall merit, I think, a comfort, somehow. Let humanity think itself better than it is—they have time to learn.

I am woken by the quiet tapping of wood. I blink and roll. I hear the tapping again, soft as a call in the night. I open the door to the storeroom where I sleep, and I find her, Lister, dressed in a smock like mine. She has tied faded ribbons in her hair.

'Say the word,' she says, 'and I am gone.'

She takes my hand in hers and presses it; at her touch I begin to tremble. I feel the heat rising in me. Her eyes meet mine. I am astonished by her—I did not think her so bold. But she is a creator, and timidity creates nothing. She reaches for me, lays her hand on my cheek, draws me to her. I shiver like autumn leaves at the breath of winter, but her breath is hot—so hot—so close.

'Stay.'

I wake to the tramp of footsteps and rise out of a languor which has no right to exist outside the height of summer. Lister sleeps beside me, her breathing soft and rhythmic. There is some new quality to the air, some strange sense in which I have been changed. I rise.

They have come to wake me and the others who will take the dead. It is my night to drive. We are in a storeroom where the blankets and clothes of the dead are kept, laundered and re-used for the tending of the sick. It is a messy business, and we do not have cloth to spare. This room is transformed too, by our touch: we have made it ours, if only for an hour. I dress and find a jug. I slip down to where the water is stored—the buckets brought this morning have been refilled many times.

I fill the jug. I splash water between my thighs and rub. Though I am sore and tired, I am newer than I have ever been. What simple power rests in her hands! My being has been impressed with the marks of those quick and clever fingers.

She is dressed when I return, and shy. She is dressed in a man's clothes and, though she has rolled the pants and pinched the shirt, I should not have known her from a distance. She offers me a matching set and tells me her plan. I listen. I feel myself quiver. My hands shake. Then I nod.

I saunter, stomp and stride—I take up space and I growl like a beast. The other women start when they see us, but I say we are from the General, and they do not question us. They help me to harness the wagon, then bring out the horses. All the time their eyes do not rise to meet mine.

They do not question that one of us walks with a stick, or that we have come at all. *Such power!* I think, in a suit of clothes. I urge the horses on. I sit—knees wide apart—and the women look away. I shiver at the thrill of it—this power, forbidden to me. Could I now pass through a crowd like a shadow—exciting neither look nor remark? Could I pass by the soldiers and find them friends? What freedom they have! This whole city is theirs—theirs to strut about and own.

I find myself wanting to pull one of the women off to the side, just to see what would happen. When no-one could see us, I would pull open my shirt. *See? See?* I would say. *I am just like you!*

Their power and freedom is nothing but posture and cloth. Let us rise up—and teach them to respect us!

But I do not. I grunt and urge the horses on. Lister and I encounter nothing—no-one stops or questions us. I am used to being challenged by every soldier in the city. This quiet—it is alien.

We pass out through the main gates. I urge the horses on, directing them upland, while Lister takes off her hat. She turns her face up to the scatter-shot stars and laughs. She laughs into the bitter breath of winter, laughs into the deadening snow, and takes out her ribbons and threads them through her hair. They stream in the wind. *Home!* she seems to cry, *At last, I am going home!*

THE SECRET OF ETHR

Alex Lee

Jamie opens his eyes to the fresh light of early morning. Vetch isn't there, but there's cooking gear propped on xyr pack. It's rained in the night; fern fronds are beaded with droplets and the earth smells damp. The anxiety he was carrying yesterday has gone. His mind feels clear like the sparkle of the fallen rain. Vetch returns with a handful of berries and fungus, sees him and smiles.

'You sleep sound?'

Jamie remembers waking only once in the night and feeling Vetch's body tucked up warm beside him.

'Sure did,' he smiles back.

'I'm making breakfast. Why don't you wash?' As Vetch passes xe touches Jamie behind the ear, like xe used to when they woke together.

After they've eaten, they return to the prospector's camp site. It's a still life tableau: last night's dinner plates and empty liquor cups scattered round a burnt-out fire, bed-roll and pack bundled into a backrest, dew steaming off the rock in the morning sun. And the prospector's body, slumped forward and fixed forever in that position, petrified.

Wrong place, wrong time. Poor fucker, Jamie thinks. But the guy's face shows contentment; the quartz flecks on his cheekbones are catching the light.

Vetch ferrets through the gear, sorting what to leave, what to take and what to destroy. Jamie chips off a bit of the body, runs the sample through the analyser and types his message:

> 8.07am 20 December 2256
> Target geo-neutralised. Sample to verify. Camp and body intact. Company property destroyed. Agent 2WB heading west via Delf. Expected arrival at checkpoint 6 days.

'Do you think they'll buy it?' Vetch asks.

'Maybe.' Jamie does a last check of the site and shoulders his pack. 'Depends on what they know and how sure they need to be. If they don't gen-test the body, it should pass for yours, I guess.'

'I'll feel better when I've got us both into the caves.' Vetch turns and leads the way down the hill.

They pick a path through the undergrowth. It's thick in some places, so they follow the fallen trunks where they can. Jamie watches his friend as they walk. Xyr shoulders are broader now, and xyr dark curls are threaded with grey.

Vetch breaks the silence. 'Did you know it was me you were hunting?'

'Only that I was looking for an earthmapper—with valuable company intellectual property.'

For years, they'd worked together as a surveying team for the company. Vetch would feel into the ground to find the rich seams of palladium, plutonium, gold. But it was fine work and had a maximum range of about 20 kilometres—so xe needed to know where to look, and that was Jamie's job. They'd hang around in prospector camps and satellite towns, Vetch listening and talking, Jamie sensing the emotions hidden behind the words. It could be slow. Months of just waiting, following the lines of people's fear and anger. Sometimes they got tangled up in someone's drama—the knots of co-dependence, addiction and violence that bound people who had no opportunities and had run out of hope. The alliances of state and big business made the conditions that ruined people's lives. Vetch and Jamie were part of that system, extending its reach and power. They could do nothing, because they were bound to it. Indentured labour. Their debt was for the surgical interventions that had made their bodies and the constant supply of biochemicals they needed to live as who they were.

'When I didn't hear from you, I thought something had happened,' Jamie continues. *That whole time and no word.* He speaks the last thought in his head.

'I had to set things up before I could try,' Vetch says.

'What things?'

Silence. *Xe's not ready, and there's no point in pushing it.* Jamie feels a surge of anger. But that's just the crest of his feelings; there's a mixture of hurt and grief in the swell. He concentrates on the stamp of his feet and the scents of the earth.

They come to a thrutch cut in the land by a creeklet. Vetch eases down one bank, then jumps the distance to the other, sinking xyr fingers into the ferns to steady xemself. Jamie follows, and they scramble up and keep walking.

'You know this forest?' asks Jamie.

'It's temperate rainforest, typical of these parts of Majeste.' Vetch loves plants.

'What are the names of the trees?' It's a game they used to play on the road.

'I'll try to remember,' xe laughs.

They walk through the morning, stopping for more food on the southern face of a ridge. Their meal is oak sorrel, mushrooms, walnut bread and the last of the berries.

'Are you going to tell me?' Jamie asks.

'What?'

'Why we're running.'

Vetch swallows xyr mouthful. 'It's a lot. And you can't share it. If we separate, I mean.'

'I don't want to separate.' *Not like I can just walk back into my job anyway*, Jamie thinks.

'You might when you hear.'

'No. I won't.' They look at each other, like they're searching for something. Jamie feels his defiance soften into tenderness. *Same eyes, deep dark brown.* Vetch looks away.

'I went to Hord following a lead. Tehir is its pre-colonial name. Remember that subnet group? They gave me a contact. Someone who would know.'

'Know what?'

'About how the Maj empire started. It wasn't always like it is now.'

The colonial history they'd learned at school hadn't interested Jamie. A bunch of names and dates. The Majestans' travelling and trade routes; lists of goods and places they had to remember. The discovery of new lands and the great men who'd found them, set up the early commercial partnerships then innovated governance. It was just the dead weight of his heritage. Depressing and stifling, like a visit to his grandparents. For Vetch, though, it had been like a puzzle, something with a secret hidden somewhere in it.

'It took time. I had to build relationships. It helped that I remembered a bit of the language. And that I showed them this.' Vetch tapped the back of xyr neck, where xe had the tattoo of a leaf. It was a mark of xyr Hordian immigrant status.

Xyr family had fled Hord when xe was only four. They'd come to Majeste because the old colonial power had a humanitarian program for Hordian immigrants. Vetch's family had lived in an offshore processing facility for six months, until xyr parents were indentured to a botanicals plant and xe was sent to the company school. It was where they sent the special kids—of which there were many among the Hordians—and where xe met Jamie.

'The mining contract had us all working long hours, but the company didn't watch us so hard. They didn't want to offend their hosts. We got leave to explore on our days off. I'd been told to hang around in the market in Kenna, get to know people first. Had to be real patient. But how could they trust me? Eventually someone said they'd take me to meet my contact. Ey was a librarian. Had these papers hidden away in the roof.'

'This is the key.' Vetch touches xyr neck again. 'This leaf. Ethr. It was part of Tehirian culture.' Xe pauses. 'They used it to Fix their bodies.'

'What was wrong with them?'

'Nothing. I mean to keep their bodies in the same form. The Tehir call it Fixing.'

'Same form as what?'

'Our bodies used to change. Flexible, like our minds. They weren't fixed in basic morphology like they are now.'

'I don't understand.'

Vetch stops to think. Xe hasn't worked out how to say this to anyone.

'You know how our bodies start to change, after deep sensing or mapping?'

'Yeah, but that's just our instability. Our genetics are weaker than other people.'

'No. That's just what they told us.' Vetch pauses. 'The world is not what they said. *We* are not what they said. Everyone's bodies used to change like ours do, but more. Completely.'

Jamie frowns. 'Completely? You mean like back and forth, man to woman?'

'No. Like only change. There was no 'man' and 'woman'. The Tehirians used the ethr leaf to capture individual states for a short time. They have over a thousand words for all the different body states. It's in their cosmology.'

'Were they—?' Jamie stops short. Ashamed at the persistence of his Maj racism.

'Human? Of course. Their bodies were the same as ours in structure, just in constant flux. What we call man and woman were just two forms. When the Maj found the ethr and saw what it could do they saw a way they could institute a new order. They were only traders back then.'

'They fixed everyone's bodies? Everyone? Permanently?' Jamie demands.

'They isolated the active ingredient, stabilised it. Everyone gets a shot in utero and another at birth. The bini vacc, remember? Most times it fixes the body into 'man' or 'woman', but for some of us, it doesn't work so well. That's why you and I need the genochems. Our bodies are more like humans used to be.'

'That's crazy.'

'I know how it sounds, but—'

'Wait, so what about sex?'

'What do you mean, sex?'

'Reproduction. Is that not real?' Vetch hears the edge in Jamie's voice and remembers the shock xe felt too.

'That's real.' Xe speaks gently. 'It's the gender part. Typing people by two sets of genitals. And only two. Building a whole system on that. Tehir wasn't like that. And the Maj as people weren't like that either.'

There's a long silence. Vetch watches xyr friend's face as he tries to process this information.

'I can't believe it. It would mean… I don't even know!' Jamie bursts out.

'I can show you the documents I brought back.'

'No. Not now.' Jamie is frowning at the patch of ground in front of him, and looks up into Vetch's eyes.

'Hey, I'm still with you. I just need some time.' Jamie reaches out an open hand. Vetch grasps it and pulls off the armoured glove, tossing it aside. Xyr hand is warm to the touch.

'Are you?'

'Yes, Vikja.' Jamie ventures this remnant of their old intimacy.

Vetch breathes out slowly and xyr grip on Jamie's hand softens.

'Visti, Vikja, Wician, Wechseln,' xe says softly. The alternative forms of xyr name in Sanskrit, Old Norse, Old English and German. They'd discovered etymology at school together and used it to make their own, secret language.[16]

'Changing, to bend, to yield, to switch,' Jamie finishes the sequence.

'Iacobus, the coloniser.' Vetch smiles. Xyr eyes are gentle and xyr hand's touch feels like a caress.

The forest noises are clear and crisp. Jamie can hear the silences between them.

I'll come apart if xe touches me, he thinks.

The lines xyr fingers trace split the skin and Jamie's body opens into parts. The outermost layer, a hard carapace, floats up and away, carried by a gentle breeze, and disappears into the forest. This is his cyborg body. Most sensors have them to help them channel other people's feelings. They make their own, so each is distinctive.

The next layer is peeling off under Vetch's hands—strips of leather toughened by long use. Xe clears them away, pushing them into the leaves. Beneath this is a weave of hair. A thick pelt. Jamie feels xyr fingers through the fur, kneading his ribs and pressing into the muscles of his abdomen. As this layer loosens, he can feel it slip against his outer skin. A shiver runs up his breastbone and down into his groin. He gasps. The old pelt is heaped beside them now. It holds the shape of Jamie's left shoulder and hip, but the other side is rolled in on itself. As he lets out a breath, so does the little heap. It's gathering itself up into an animal shape; a round

---

[16] Vetch, or *Vicia sativa*, is a drought-resistant plant of the pea family which is often considered a weed. It is also the name of an online journal of trans poetry, and as such recognises the hardiness of trans folk, our experiences of marginalisation and our ubiquity: http://www.vetchpoetry.org/

back, hunched shoulders, stocky limbs. The creature starts to move off toward the forest and Jamie closes his eyes. His outer skin is roughened by the rubbing and wear of the upper layers, but Vetch can feel the contours of muscles well defined. One hand on Jamie's sternum, xe reaches back to grab xyr brush, the one xe uses to take dirt off xyr gear.

Xe turns back and passes it over Jamie's chest. Increasing the pressure, xe moves the brush in arcs over the other's pecs, then traces down the line of ribs and over the curve of hipbone to rest in the flush of hair at Jamie's groin. Vetch hears xyr own breath quicken. Still working the brush, xe twists to position one knee then the other against Jamie's thighs, straddling him. Xe braces xyr legs and leans forward to run the brush again over pecs and shoulders and down Jamie's flanks, xyr free hand resting on his belly.

As xe repeats the action, the scores the brush fibres are making in the outer skin multiply and deepen, and it starts to lift away like thick paper. Xe makes xyr last sweep and brings the brush to the hollow at the top of Jamie's leg, pressing it to the tender part inside his left thigh. Xe pauses there, and passes xyr other hand back up Jamie's length and down again. The broken outer skin crinkles under the firm strokes, and as xe pushes it aside, Vetch contacts the inner layer, the living skin of Jamie's body.

Xe feels its heat and pulsing aliveness. A ripple runs through xem, like bubbles bursting beneath xyr skin. Xe lets xemself sit now and presses into Jamie, two hands on his shoulders holding him down. There's a hum of energy between their bodies.

OPEN POEM TO [redacted], MP

Tobi Evans

Dear [redacted],
I am inflamed
beyond language
to see
'WOMEN DON'T
HAVE PENISES ♥'
stamped, smug
down High Street
ten minutes
from my home.

I scratch them out
in animal rage
keys in fist
fist becomes keys
molten mettle.

I return home to find
your election pamphlet
strewn with rainbow flag
and LGB Progress™
in my letterbox.

I google you
halfway through writing this poem
in case I am being unfair
and I find one
Transgender Awareness Week
post from [redacted], 2021
celebrating

free trans health care
at [redacted] Health.

One month after
your PA wrote this Content®
[redacted] Health ran out of
Trans Doctors©
and wouldn't allow me
to see 'A Normal Doctor'
for a new surgery referral
one month from an admission.

Two months later
I waited 40 minutes
for a nurse
who was not there.
Reception Apologised
showed me the Complaint Box
but said I couldn't
see anyone else.

In my last-minute appointment
at another practice
a nurse exploded
testosterone decanoate
over both of us,
me: butt out on the table
her: 'I think I gave you half!'

At home
I called a trans nurse
who told me what to do.
Thank fuck for friends.

Together we create trans utopias
well-worn with knowledge
out of book clubs and Zoom calls
zines, four-letter names and chai.

In the system you built
we play Russian roulette with our health.
We do not win.
The average life expectancy of a trans person
is 35 years old.
I am 29 years old
too young to be an Elder.

[redacted],
You splash WOMEN'S RIGHTS
Rainbow Flags®
Aboriginal Flags
GETTING THINGS DONE™
on shiny office windows,

but the average life expectancy of a trans person
is 35 years old

and some fucker
bought a custom stamp
to tell me
I don't exist

and by the time I finish this poem
three days later
I am scratching out bullshit
again.

[redacted],
Pronouns are like arseholes
everyone has one.
We want
free trans health care
gender affirmation leave
a Royal Commission
national birth certificate sex/name change reform.
We want to live.

We have been trans
for 300,000 years

and we will be trans
until the sun runs out.

We have had Parliament
for 121 years
and you have been an MP
for [redacted] years.

Will you meet me on High Street
outside ALDI
with your keychain?

Will you meet us
at Parliament?
Will you Get Things Done™?

TRANSRAGE
Or, anger is an investment in each other

Madison Moffat, The Swamp System, Alex Lee

Winter 2022. We were talking about writing.

The world was there
at the
edges of the room.

Debating whose body can be where, doing what
Whose safety is paramount,
Whose sovereignty matters.

These words have a material *force.*
Their meanings come to life in our bodies.

Across the pulses between cells, as they travel across the nervous system, is a particular modulation which tugs and heats. The potential to strike, so far held back, is on the verge of cannibalising my will before instead switching to mental convulsion.

The president of the International Swimming Federation says, 'We have to protect the rights of our athletes to compete, but we also have to protect competitive fairness at our events, especially the women's category…'[17]

Prior trauma and points of fierce contention, hitherto suspended, lunge to mentally merge with the contingency immediately before me. I am consumed with indignation and fear. My self becomes anger-self, a mode of relation that can spur positive change or scorch earth.

The US supreme court justice says: 'Roe was egregiously wrong from the start. Its reasoning was exceptionally weak, and the decision has had damaging consequences. […] It is time to heed the Constitution and return the issue of abortion to the people's elected representatives.'[18]

Anger is the fire that licks and claws in my throat, sometimes tenderly requesting to be breathed out and others ripping and tearing its way through my oesophagus. It lingers in the air, lurking, waiting for the right moment to strike. It burns and bubbles away with every 'she' and 'no'. Anger is inside of me, and I don't hate it. In fact I welcome the rush and release it offers me when I know I have to face the losing battle that is life.

The defence lawyer for the officer charged with the murder of a young Aboriginal man calls the death a tragedy but finds the victim accountable for the violence that unfolded. He, not the police officer, is responsible for his own death.

My anger begins with my father—the grandson of a man who nearly beat another to death outside a public house. Over the top of that violence and rage a class-aspirant respectability was constructed. My father spoke the words of righteousness and reason to sanction his fears, confusions and aggressions. He derided everyone who was different, most proximately his wife and children. This anger has now lodged in me. In it are the memories of working-class men and dominated women—a knot of antipathy at the centre of the heteronormative family roped into the

[17] https://www.fina.org/news/2649715/press-release-fina-announces-new-policy-on-gender-inclusion
[18] https://www.supremecourt.gov/opinions/21pdf/19-1392_6j37.pdf

colonising mission, propping themselves with fantasies of whiteness. It burns in my chest, crackles on my skin, hollows out my throat; an ouroboros[19] in fury devouring.

The conservative politician in the year of an election says: 'They want to capture children and adolescents as profit centres by promoting hormonal and surgical gender transition as a solution for emotional distress and social awkwardness, and remove basic safeguarding for children and women.'[20]

The other is truly other; but we can still understand each other through knowing what we jointly will never stand by. Anger serves to ward off the vanguards of nice, who wilfully or unwittingly perpetuate and sanction impositions that are not aimed their way. Anyone can be nice; it is kindness that takes effort. Burning frustration, even terror, can be shared with mutually kind others; and this can collectively call upon us to gather and declare our care and concern. The opposite of anger is not love, it is indifference. I am angry primarily because I am invested. Mutually emoted anger is an investment in each other. The severely marginalised can still defy encompassing and contiguous apathy: 'I matter, and I refuse to abide by X. I will justly retaliate if necessary.

Our anger interacts with the world by giving us the strength to hold it on our shoulders. It helps us express and explore every nook and cranny of life—those that most try to stop us from reaching.

---

[19] An ancient symbol, the ouroboros depicts a serpent or dragon eating its own tail.
[20] https://www.theguardian.com/australia-news/2022/apr/14/nsw-liberal-candidate-described-campaign-supporting-lgbt-youth-as-grooming-tactic-used-by-gender-extremists

There's things you don't know; we're filled with love—love that you will never know

THE DROP

Sarah L

It was a cold morning. Freezing. Sierra cradled her coffee in her hands. Cafe Musette was pretty empty at this unearthly hour. A couple of insomniac teenagers here, some travellers taking a break from their long journey there. Just ten minutes ago a bunch of people had got back on the Greyhound to continue their journey to Sydney. She glanced at the clock. 3 am. *God. When is he going to get here?*

It'd been months since she'd been to town. The farm was two hours away, and someone else usually did the grocery runs. Not that she was a hermit; she just preferred the wide expanse of the country. She'd had enough of dingy corners and the holes in walls where she used to live. There was a time when she'd slept rough, hugging her laptop for dear life because it was her only source of income, overstaying her welcome in cafes to do her work. Fortunately she was a brilliant hacker and managed to hustle her way into some well-paid gigs that enabled her to climb out of the hole she'd been thrown into.

But that was five years and a very long time ago. When her family kicked her out of the house after she came out. Suffering years of crippling dysphoria that nearly killed her. After the Deves victory and the incumbent stayed in power, everything went downhill fast.

She had spent the first few months couch surfing, glad of the friends who were willing to take her in. But the support and patience wore thin, and she knew when she was no longer welcome. The first year was tough. She'd tried the homeless shelters, but not many were prepared to take in someone like her. The increasingly right-wing government meant that previously inclusive places were reluctant to extend a helping hand. Not that they'd displayed outright hostility. They were just…a little more gatekeepey.

But sleeping rough had meant it became necessary to band together. Perhaps it was a blessing in disguise, because that was how the Collective came into being. A bunch of trans and gender-diverse folks pooling resources for survival in what had come to be known as the Gender Wars. The Collective grew: the government made access to medical care a little more restrictive with every passing legislation, and this motley collection of artists, activists, hackers and outcasts decided to do something about it.

Connections started forming between similar groups in other cities. They found ways to bypass the state's firewall, and an underground network of smugglers and runners mobilised. And somewhere, someone decided it would be a great idea to start a camel farm in the middle of nowhere.

Which was what led her here. Albury. A border town. The birthplace of BabelJS. In a cafe beside a train station. This liminal space between states. Doing a pick-up. Not her usual gig. Also not from a person she cared to meet.

A ute pulled up in the foggy darkness. Sierra recognised the chain hanging from the rear-view mirror. She watched as the driver got out and ambled to the cafe entrance. He stood in the foyer for a few seconds. She turned around, their eyes met and he walked over before plopping himself on the seat next to her.

'Took you long enough,' she said quietly. 'You were supposed to be here an hour ago.'

'Sorry, the baby woke up. It's my turn to settle her. Mark didn't get much sleep last night,' Stan replied.

Sierra felt the familiar pangs, knowing she could never have children. She stuffed it down. *There are more important things to deal with here.* 'You got the stuff?'

'No,' said Stan, 'They've been watching the airstrip. We're bringing it in another way. It'll arrive next week.'

While they weren't exactly restricted substances, hormones had been harder to come by in recent years. Even though there was no outright ban, the bigoted Right had made access much more difficult for gender-diverse people. And there were fewer doctors willing to prescribe them. Every year, a few more of them dropped off the radar.

'The Guild's not going to be happy. We've got a backlog of people waiting for their 'mones.' Sierra took a gulp of her coffee.

'Why are we even meeting up anyway? You should have cancelled this.'

Stan was silent for a few seconds, then said, 'Mum wants to see you.'

'What do you mean?'

'She's dying, Sierra. We think the end could be near.'

Sierra sneered into the darkness outside. 'Well, she can keep asking. She's dead to me. Besides, aren't you the favourite? You're the one who gave them a son. Not me.'

'Look, I know the past few years have been hard on you. I know there's nothing I can do to undo all of that. But whatever happened, we're still family.'

'I have no family. They kicked me out. And don't think that you volunteering for this drop excuses the work you've done with the Gender Criticals movement. Many of us would still be alive if not for the shit they've done to us!'

Sierra gripped her cup tightly, hands trembling. *Calm down, Sierra.* She took a sip of the now tepid coffee, swallowing down mouthfuls of bitter memory. *Keep calm.*

Gulp.

Keep down the memory of loss, helplessness and despair the night she was cast out and her brother did nothing.

Gulp.

That time she woke up in the middle of the night on Mike's sofa bed, listening to him trying to reason with his partner.

'What do you want me to do, Trent? He's got nowhere to go.'

'I don't want a tranny in our house!'

Gulp.

Getting turned away at the homeless shelter.

Gulp.

The time she had to turn to Premarin when other options ran out.

Fuck the cis!

Keep it down…

Push it down, Sierra. Keep it down.

'Look, I know I can't undo what happened,' Stan intoned quietly, pulling her back to the present. 'But I'm trying to do what I can to help now.'

Sierra looked at his reflection on the glass, against the night. Hands gripped tight, slumped shoulders. Yes, he's sorry. But so what?

'It's too little, and way too late,' Sierra muttered under her breath. 'If you're looking for forgiveness, you've come to the wrong place. If you want absolution, I suggest you build a time machine.'

'Look, your transition was hard on all of us. You know how Mum and Dad were so set on having grandkids. And after I came out, they were devastated. I'm sorry they ended up putting all their hopes on you.'

'You were always their favourite,' muttered Sierra. 'You were always the standard shitty older brother until after I came out.' Except instead of becoming less shitty, he'd become her main tormentor.

She pulled up her left sleeve, exposing a long, brown keloid on her forearm. 'This is what you and your friends did to me,' she said. The day she ran away, Stan and a group of his mates had cornered her and beaten her up. The gash on her arm came from a rusty nail stuck to a piece of fence one of them decided to hit her with.

Stan was silent. If he was shocked, he didn't show it.

'There's also the stab wound near my right shoulder. I was just really lucky I had a place to go to. I wouldn't be here otherwise.'

Sierra started putting her stuff into her backpack. There was no response worth waiting for. Fishing out her key, she said, 'If I had my way, you wouldn't be working with the Collective. And believe me, I fought against this at the council meeting. And telling my story to show you're an ally? Wow, that really takes the cake.' She stood up, slung the backpack on her shoulders and started to walk.

He's right. He can't change the past. There was nothing she could do except pick up the pieces of her life. Turning around, she said, 'Frankly, I'm not sure I can trust you. I only turned up for my people, and because there's no-one else available. You'll have to make arrangements with another Guild member for the next drop.'

With that, Sierra strode across the hall. Past the cishet couple huddled in the corner box watching YouTube, past the homeless woman taking refuge from the cold, past the waiter at the cash register.

She pushed the glass door open, put on her helmet, got on her Harley and rode out into the morning darkness.

FRAGMENTED MESS

The Swamp System

Coming into this world wasn't the best experience, though we tend to not have many of those. I don't remember all of them, but I like to think of the good things. Like just the other day. I realised who I was. Not just a fluctuation of the real one, which is what I had assumed. But a fully evolved person with my own wants and feelings, and it's such a magical feeling to be me. I have a name and my own taste in music and my own Tumblr account. This isn't something most of you see as a big deal, but I have never had anything like that. I haven't been able to exist as more than a mood or a phase.

I am real, and we are all real. We were going to write a fiction story about a multiple who must solve a crime or something, but I think this story is more important. This is our story. As told from five different perspectives. Or, as some of you might believe, one perspective.

I—I mean WE—are here to prove to you that not only do we exist but that there are so many of us out there who need to be heard, who need to be seen for who we truly are. Multiple individuals in the same body. We think, feel, speak and act just like that. Multiple people living one life. I am not what would be known as the 'host' or the 'original', but I wanted to be the first to talk because I am so passionate about this. We exist, and even though the percentage of plurals is small we still deserve to be treated with the same respect and kindness as any other individual. This is all very long and ranty, but that's how I type. That's how I AM.

We all suffer from ADHD, autism and dyslexia, but this is part of how I experience it. I'm loud and have no idea of personal space and can talk for HOURS about things I'm passionate about, and I can kind of go on and on, but I will be frank here as I only have 500 words. As mentioned, I am one part or 'alter' of a system.

The system is the body we share and the alters are the people who make up our minds. It's LOUD and hard to concentrate a lot of the time but we manage. We have OSDD1B, and what that means is we have a dissociative disorder similar to DID (Dissociative Identity Disorder). But we have one difference. We have no amnesia between parts or alters. So, we remember what each person does but we have emotional amnesia, which means I look at the memory from before I fronted (otherwise known as taking the lead) and I remember it, but I know I didn't do that.

It's all confusing; don't worry, it's confusing for us too. But each of us is coming together to show you how different and unique we all are and to hopefully reach others who feel this way, and if you are a multiple, we want you to know. YOU ARE NOT ALONE. We see you.

I float in an endless sea.

My water-soaked wings weigh me down into its depths. I breathe in the salty water and it burns my thoughts and lungs in a welcoming way. I am swallowed by nothing.

As I open my eyes, I see it.

The window into the world I call 'real'—the water pulls me up towards it and I find myself in a conversation. It takes some time to process but I know why I'm here. I'm here to serve.

But this time is different. This time they look at me. Not at me, but IN me. They see my soul and greet it fondly. They open themselves to welcome our fractured mind. I feel something I have never felt. I feel…seen. I feel heard. And I'm no longer the mimic, the actor, the other.

I'm me.

I'm real and they not only acknowledge me but love me for it. I have never felt so many emotions at once. I am not the host. But I am me and we are us; just as you are real so am I. Breath never felt so real. I feel myself drifting back and instead of this dark empty ocean, I'm sitting at a warm, welcoming fire surrounded not by nothing, but by friends, and loved ones. We are many but we work as one. I am so grateful to be part of this system. I'm grateful for my friends and partners. I'm grateful to this community for expecting me. I am me and for once in our entire life. We are not only seen. But safe. Safe from the things that lurk in the darkest crevasses of the world. I may be scared and fractured. But for once I feel whole and…happy.

I am happy.

Ok, let's get some fucken facts straight. Terminology time baby!

Let's start with what I am. A fictive. Fictives are alters that are formed by their source material. They can be anything from superheroes to original characters. Yes, we are fucken real and we have our own thoughts and feelings. Fictives can be exactly like their source or, like me, very loosely similar. In my case, the only real things I have in common with my source are the fucken name and what our roles in our systems are (we get the shit done that the rest don't want to or don't have the stomach for). Fictives can have something called 'source trauma'. That's when they have trauma from what happened to them in their source material. We are real and we are valid no matter how much or how little we have in common with our source.

Factive, similar to fictive, is an introject (an alter that is created from an external source), but instead of being based on a fictional story, they are created based on a real-life person. Both fictives and factives are very common in systems that also have autism or ADHD.

APNs (apparently normal parts) are the alters that don't hold any trauma and are in charge of doing daily tasks like socialising or studying or doing your nine to five.

EPs (emotional parts) are the alters that are made to hold specific traumas or stress. Every system is fucken unique so each person has a different amount of each, but more commonly OSDD systems will have one ANP and multiple EPs (this isn't the case for us; we have multiple ANPs).

There are many different types of alters, ranging from humans to even animals of all different shapes and sizes and ages and genders. Some alters identify with the body, some don't. People can also use different terms for the word 'alter', such as parts or head-mates, and all are just a term for the individuals that make up a system.

Littles and middles are terms used for the kid alters. Usually a little is any younger kid alter, whereas middles are middle schoolers to teens.

Disassociation is when you feel disconnected from reality and in a sense drift off. You feel almost like you're seeing everything in third person, or you feel like the world around you is a fucken blur. You can feel almost like the world isn't real (also known as derealisation) or you can feel like your body is wrong or not yours (and that's known as depersonalisation).

Fragments are alters that were created for holding one specific memory or can be made for one specific purpose (like to cook or clean up).

The inner world is the place where all the alters who aren't fronting or co-conscious hang. It's a place in your mind that can look vastly different depending on the person. For example, it can be a beach or a house or a floating island. It's what you see when you close your eyes and look inward. Not all systems have an inner world, and many have to build theirs over time using meditation techniques and possibly therapy. Also, even non-systems can have inner worlds. For us, we didn't really have one—it was more of nothingness—but now we have a bonfire (not much but it's something).

Co-conscious is when an alter is watching what the person fronting is doing but is only watching and doesn't have control of the body. Also, fuck sorry I should explain fronting. Fronting is when an alter—or in the case of co-fronting, multiple alters—are in control of the body, doing all the normal stuff like walking and talking (or in my case typing). While an alter is near the front they can do something called passive influence, which is where they influence the front with either a thought or a feeling.

When an alter is dormant it means they are deep in the subconscious and not currently present in the headspace at all. Alters can go dormant for many reasons and can stay dormant for anywhere from a few hours to years.

Switching is when one alter switches with another. This can be experienced in a numerous amount of ways from fast, disorienting switches where you're thrown to the front and you have no clue how you got there to long, dissociative switches that can at worst take a few hours and feel like gloopy, blurry shit (not fun, I promise you). But not all switches are bad; some can take a few minutes and be an easy switch. Some people will say they're feeling switchy when they feel a switch coming on.

Blurry is when you can't tell who the fuck is fronting and you're just a blur of multiple alters or just have no clue who you are due to dissociation.

Splitting is a term used to explain when a new alter is formed.

Now here is the bit that is misunderstood. Most people think there is one goal for being a system. And that is known as merging. This is where all the alters merge and the person becomes a single (or as the plural community refers to them, a singlet). This is a valid and great option for some people and is something that takes time and therapy. It is a completely valid option for a lot of people to live a happy life—BUT it is not the only option, as most think. There is also something called healthy multiplicity. Healthy multiplicity is where you get therapy to help work through your trauma and accept and work through any memories that are hidden from you and live a happy, healthy life as a multiple. This also takes time, communication and therapy, but it is just as valid as final fusion (completely fusing all alters together). Also, it's important to know that there is a multitude of variations of fusing. Some alters can choose to fuse into one, and it's not an all-or-nothing situation.

Hope all that helps people to get a better understanding of what we are and what the terms we use mean! Cheers and have a good one.

Hellow! I wanted to write something. I'm what would be known as a middle. I like Pokémon and *Steven Universe* songs. I'm also known as an age slider. That means my age moves from middle to little depending on what is happening. I think a lot of this stuff is seen as scary and bad, and a lot of it is. It's scary not knowing what is happening, and bad things are scary. I don't like when bad things happen to us, but it's okay because we aren't alone. We have each other, and everyone we know now is very nice! I really, really hope you're having a good day—and just know if bad things happen, no matter if you are a single or a plural you are never alone! There are so many who are here for you! Thank you for reading my message. I hope you have a good day!

I'm the host and I'll be concluding this piece. It took a lot of time to get all of this together, 'cause switches aren't always something we can control, which makes things a bit more difficult. I'm not expecting much from this, but if we can get our story out there and help someone understand this and possibly help take the steps to make this something that becomes normalised and accepted, that would be my only wish.

This is a hard thing to deal with, but it is such a normal way for the brain to react to trauma. When you are young, before you fully develop, your mind has different parts. And when you reach around seven your mind forms into a singular personality. But when trauma happens before that, it can cause your self to stay separated, with amnesia barriers.

We went through a lot of stuff, and with each traumatic event the brain just keeps splitting. At least that's the case for traumagenic systems. (That just means a system and alters caused due to trauma, whereas endogenic systems are due to other reasons, and mixed is where you have a mix of alters formed by trauma and alters formed by other means. We do not know too much about endogenic systems.)

We found out about our plurality semi-recently, and the lack of any support in Australia is such a huge issue and left us feeling alone. There is one great support group in all of Australia, and within the New South Wales area (which is where we are from) there is little to no available therapy and no support. We want to change that. We are working to find and support the community so no-one else has to feel so alone and feel so wrong. We want to help plurals know they aren't alone. They are valid and they are valuable—you deserve love and respect and all the support you need.

I hope this gives you some insight into a community you might not have known even existed. We are many and we are proud, and we hope to give a platform to those who deserve it.

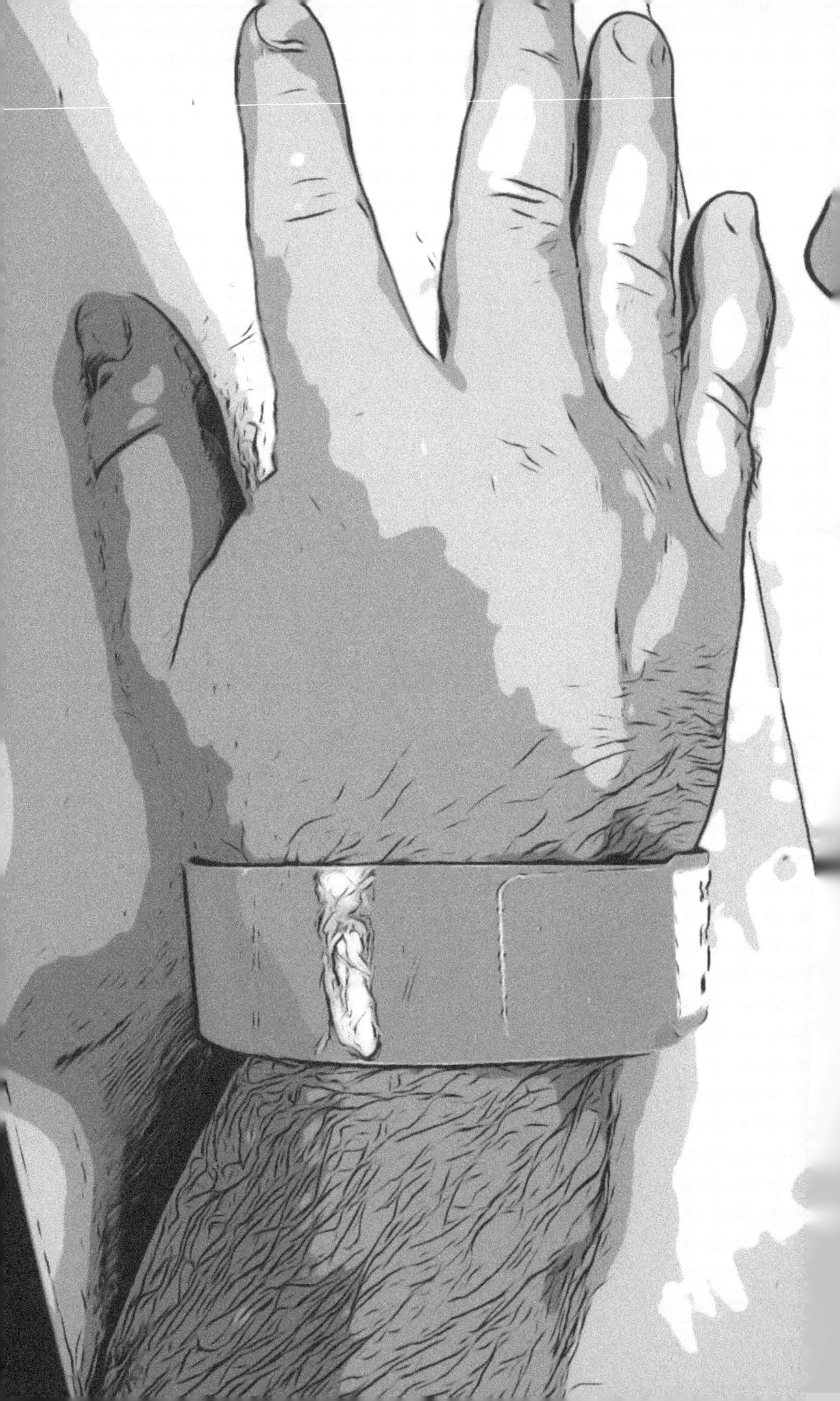

SELF-CARE TRILOGY

David Azul

The basic units of life

Over the decades, I have become very sensitive to attempts at distinguishing into kinds seemingly everything that is. When I say sensitive, I mean a mixture of attraction, desire, compulsion, fear, panic, pain, shame, disgust, avoidance, denial, repulsion and exasperation that constitutes my average way of being in the world.

It seems to me as if living one's life means to brachiate through the thicket of ever-changing customs of how one needs to present in order to be considered for membership of the acceptable. As soon as one's body is not strong enough anymore to stay aloof or to push aside what is thrown into one's way, one drops onto the asphalt that provides the stability and smooth surface for human society to run its course.

Unlike raindrops, which may multiply upon impact and eventually disperse into the ground or float up into the sky, whenever I have lost my oomph and have come into contact with the so-called 'concrete reality', I have found myself broken up into a myriad of shards, seemingly following a law of nature whose details have become buried in the dust of the everyday.

These shards reliably reopen the many wounds that cover the broken skin of my selfhood. Again and again, an army of neutrophils, macrophages, fibroblasts and other agents of destruction and reconstruction kick off the perpetual process of healing in which destroyed or damaged tissue is replaced by a reassembled matrix of the basic units of life.

The wristband

I am sitting in my room, which is currently located at a psychiatric hospital, and look at my wrist. It is encircled by a red band that came to me via a number of detours. At first, I was not given one, and I thought: I can't believe my luck! They let me continue practising my undercover agency in the community! For those of you who don't know, 'community' is the term they use to refer to the space and the people who live their lives outside the hospital, as if there was no community within and the building and its residents did not belong to the community without.

But then, my sensitivity flared up like a siren, and one of the student nurses rushed to my room, numerous wristbands in their jittery hand. They grabbed one and asked me if I wanted it strapped on tightly or loosely. I appreciated the question. 'Loosely,' I said, and a bit too loosely it was put on. The wristband fell to the ground as soon as the student had left my room. When I picked it up, I realised that I was getting involved in a case of mistaken identity. The entries on the band referred to a 24-year-old by the name of Camilla Bland. I was tempted to put the new wristband on and see if it would allow me to live my life in the hospital as a different person, taking their medications, eating their food and wearing their clothes.

But this fantasy was only short-lived, because I knew that wristbands are not normally consulted for identification purposes in the hospital's everyday life. Just as in the outside world, people who wander the corridors within tend to refer to and treat each other based on their own imaginations of who the other might or should be and what their needs and wishes are.

My thoughts were interrupted by a knock at my door. The student had returned to apologise profusely and hand me the wristband they believed I should wear. I scanned the entries on the new band urgently, just as I would do in the supermarket checking ingredient lists on food items to identify potential allergens. As it has become second nature to me, I rated my distress on a scale from 5 (= the minimum level of alarm I tend to experience when going about my everyday life) to 10 (= full-blown crisis). My self-rating hovered around 5 while I checked if the names and the date of birth on the band matched the information I tend to divulge about myself for official purposes. Then a jump to the perfect storm of 10/10 when I caught sight of one of the parents of all categorisations: gender.

Flashbacks of previous misidentifications intruded into my mind: when I had to practise beam routines and needlework instead of soccer and woodwork in the Catholic primary school I was enrolled in for four years; when I was called to the starting block to participate in gender-segregated swimming competitions; when I was greeted by my analyst at the entrance to her clinic every second day of the week; when hairdressers refused to cut my hair how I wanted it to be and in the section of the shop where I wanted to sit; when medical personnel popped their heads into crowded waiting zones to call me up as the next person in line. After all these years, I still bend my head in shame, as if the whiff of gender branding has emerged from my rotten core.

This time, it was the so-called 'other' gender with which the person in the nurse uniform was trying to tie me up. Instead of holding out my wrist limply as if I accepted the makeshift trinket with grace, I took possession of the piece of plastic that was supposed to represent me, threw it in the bin and replaced it with my tag that marks me as myself.

Who are you today?

The waiting zone of a university voice clinic is a good spot to encounter the instability of classifications of all sorts. It is the space where new students wait to meet their clinical educator for the first time, where clients gather as well as significant others. I even saw the head of school once waiting to pick up a research subject. Sometimes I sit there, too, to catch my breath on a busy day. Embarrassing confusions happen regularly: a carer is mistaken for her client's son; a new client for the supervisor, for the long-awaited service technician, for a human resource officer, for a new colleague. 'Brothers and sisters' turn out to be couples, 'couples' mother and son, the 'bad wig' all the rage from London. I would be lost for words and appropriate address if it weren't for our receptionist, who holds the clue. She will give me the covert hints I need to rebuild my clinical world.

I put my name badge on my shirt and approach the person the receptionist has pointed out to me. Over the years, I have practised how to take control of misunderstandings by telling the waiting zone people quickly and firmly who I am and what my position is. I am the clinical supervisor, the one who will observe the student clinicians and the clients in their encounters. I am the big brother and not the namby-pamby nancy boy I might have been seen as in the seconds before I opened my mouth to set things straight. Then my students appear from behind me and ostensibly take over the lead. I disappear into the video observation room, from where I can zoom in on every session and capture all that is said and shown for later analysis. From a comfortable distance I pursue my supervisory business. Untouchable, inviolable, objective.

This is neither how it is nor how I want it to be. The one-way mirror technologies in the observation room prove to be an insubstantial illusion the more time I spend alone in my black box. Instead of looking through the layers of pane at the client and the student clinicians, I often find myself focusing on my reflection in the mirror. Instead of the client's story it is as if my voice comes out of the speaker retelling aspects of my life in changing versions and variable accentuations. I recognise desperation and struggle welling up the cables and rocking the membranes. There are exaggerated expectations of possibilities for change side by side with merciless self-hate and devaluation of body shapes and functions. But I can also hear amazed appreciation of achieved improvements, and savour the busy humming of confidence and resilience.

Soundless tears are sliding over my face while my students and their client are having a laugh. They are looking at pictures the client brought, showing apparently different members from her family, but as she tells us, they are all her: the crying little child with the doll in its hands, the dark-haired, bearded youngster with flared trousers and a long collared shirt next to a Volkswagen bus, the large office worker in a three-piece suit sitting at a desk sharpening a pencil and the blonde lady in the pink dress with the serious expression and the briefcase in her hand. As further evidence the client loosens her blouse from her skirt, lifts it and points at scars on her stomach. This is where she had her liposuction surgery done, because of which she cannot do her breathing exercises properly: the skin is so tight that it doesn't allow for movements of her belly. Then she points at her face and says that she is having a whole-body laser epilation at the moment and that she covers the remnants of her stubble with make-up. The students join the client in her controlled laughter, which drowns out any potential overtones of injury, vulnerability or doubt.

I encountered the presence of sadness in my own story first in the shape of tears in my counsellor's eyes. I appreciated the inviting gesture but found myself too concerned about the spontaneous break with the unspoken rule of 'clinicians don't cry' to be able to join in. Maybe it is easier to cry on behalf of the other than to admit that one grieves for oneself?

When I tasted my tears in the video observation room I thought: it is as if I am at the same time supervising and playing a part in a staging of my autobiography. As with the client's photos, there seem to be various actors involved, but in reality, I am the only performer. I feel demoralised to witness a repetition of the conditions I found unbearable myself. I am appalled at the normative forces I teach my students to apply, just as I was taught decades ago during my own training in speech pathology. It gives me the creeps to see the clients comply with procedures that normalise processes of standardisation, just as I followed my treatment regime as prescribed, according to the rules of the 'standards of care for gender identity disorders'. I am overwhelmed with the effects of reviewing what I had done to me, who I have become and who I am not anymore.

If I have a look at my photos all spread out on the table, it is like picking up the shards from a vase that has just fallen on a tiled floor. Holding those sharp fragments in my hand is difficult to do without cutting myself. The memories that are kicking off don't make a smooth story, an entity, an identity. I can't sense the coherence other people seem to embody so easily. I feel like a stranger to myself when looking at what is supposed to represent me.

There is 'Peter', a bare-chested boy in blue shorts running along a gravel road through a Swedish forest. His hair is blown out of his eager face, leaving a woman and a girl a little behind. Later he is stirring a camp fire on the beach with a stick, his face red from the heat and the excitement.

Here I can see 'Anna Sirene Blume', a long-haired, drunk youngster playing the guitar on a bed where other youths are gathered. She is spending some time in Poland writing a paper on the devastating environmental situation there, which she is determined to improve at a later stage. Along the way she is exploring the different brands of Polish vodka and her repertoire of flower power songs.

Next I come across 'DJ Azul', with dreadlock spikes, a very broad smile and a techno outfit, chilling out on a balcony with friends.

There are no pictures and no names for the trespassers in my life: the naked woman, her legs widely spread apart, her hair hanging greasily and dull from her blank face, her head bent and drawn to the ground, like the hanging body fat and her huge breasts; the ragged, emaciated person, hearing voices, caught up in soliloquy, wandering the streets aimlessly; the adult who occasionally shrinks to become a child with all the insecurities and feelings of guilt, shame and inexperience that come with this metamorphosis; the dreamer with the supernatural powers specialised in walking at ceiling height in the air above everybody else.

How can one assume that it would be the right thing to squeeze into one kind of human all of those different ways of relating to and being in the world?

How could one expect to come upon one voice with harmonious characteristics for all those impersonations?

How dare one order everybody to sing the same song?

When I come and see my singing teacher, her cordial voice sounds as if she asks: 'Who are you today?' And then I choose between the march, the *Lied*, the blues, silence or something else in order to create the space to become the 'I' for the night.

INDELIBLE

Jordie Slonim

'Do you hold yourself accountable for ANY of this?' I asked.

I perched with my bum towards the front third of this seat, ample space between my tensed back and the back of the armchair. My feet were touching the floor, writhing, one ball of foot over the top of my other toes. A feeble attempt at nervous system regulation.

She sat in that brown chair opposite me, right leg crossed over other knee, right arm crossed over her body. She did not shift from this position during what transpired.

I felt it coming. An onset of fragmentation, signalling the explicit message that I should evict myself, at least in part, from my body. So I dissociated to allow that part to watch her from the side.

I surveilled as she began to purge. From this angle, a fascination washed over me. I observed a body that remained rigid in its furled state, whilst an accumulation of truths erupted. A collection of hidden emotions, thoughts, beliefs, assumptions about my presence in her life. I observed as every cell, blood vessel, muscle, every bone was sucked dry of the filth she felt about my existence in her life, and formed a tornado in her belly that she could no longer contain.

It unleashed. From my side-on position, I saw the words escape her body, a metaphysical representation of 'spitting nails'. That gusto of vomit washed over my body as I sat in the opposite chair. Chunks of undigested experience edging down the walls, leaving stains, with pools gathering underfoot.

I was the convenient receptor of this bile. A thousand slaps in the face that landed in such quick succession, and with such ferocity, that I am glad I was already predisposed to pre-empt those signs I should escape my body. A tirade of transgressions.

I should do this, think that, feel and behave this way. The assertion that who and how I was was an assault to her comfort.

I dared not breathe it in. Dissociation created time and space.

I whispered in my own ear, 'You did not create this on your own'.

A part of me remained in a state of allure that her body had not moved from her original position. Healthy distraction. The body became more tense; her head moved as she unloaded. Lightning belted out from her general vicinity, but it was as though the top leg was fixed to the bottom leg and her hands were glued together. Almost as though her body was attempting to keep it all contained, maintain the masked facade, but was unable to achieve its task.

I shifted my dissociated position to float behind my physical body. I looked over each of her shoulders, to gauge if there was some mystical little creature whispering in her ear, reminding her of all of these infractions she had neglected to address over the last three and a half years. Or dictating all of the things someone else had previously cited for her to declare.

Her purge was complete. A smugness emerged. A smirk, nostrils flaring, chin down a smidge. Her eyes bored holes. She was encased in an envelope of satisfaction. Back in control.

A therapeutic tool restored to take over.

That smirk shifted, lips slightly parting to verbally confirm her newly re-formed role. 'I still don't know where you're at', she said.

The dissociated self sucked themself back into physical body and disbelief roamed through every cell. Still integrating, abandoned parts re-forming to merge back, I observed the shrink's body ease out of its rigidity as the safety of her therapist self took charge. She replaced stiffness with a confidence, like she could breathe again. Both of us were re-calibrating, with our agendas blinking neon in our prefrontal cortices.

'I still don't know where you're at' served to eradicate years of a friendship connection, as we were swiftly transported back in time, into her original psychologist's room. With her embodied 'power over' status resumed, I could be seen as inferior to her again. She could be safe to mould and manipulate me back into the box of her making.

The intensity of attack subsided, sculpting into covert manoeuvres. I was conscious of her intention, and still blinding myself to it in order to refocus back to my original objective for this conversation—to salvage the friendship. My fixation was meaningless. Her body screamed, 'Fuck off out of my space, out of my clinic, out of my life'. But her mouth stayed on track with sickly-sweet prose, functioning as guidance into her ever-expanding maze of confusion, never stating what she ACTUALLY desired—for me to leave.

What words can I use to get her to verbalise her body language? How much time, how much space, how much energy, how long do I wait for her to utilise spoken word?

My futility of focus, yearning for this hollow connection to endure, kept me stuck in this web, life force drained. I fumbled and faltered and failed again and again.

The stains of her projections could not be washed off. They had seeped into my pores, absorbed into my blood flow, circulating into organ, gland, bone, chakra. Indelible.

IN THE ABSENCE OF PRESENCE

Jordie Slonim

I am absent, present, absent
Am I?
Absent to…
Are they present?

(Sigh)
I sigh
I wait
I wonder
I Trans
Apart from

I separate
Feel the gap
I disconnect
I dis-connect
Dis-lodge
Separated

I am away
I hold
A takeaway
I alone
Lone
Wait
I Trans

I don't connect
Do I connect?
I don't connect

Am I connect-ed?
(Sigh)
Empty
I miss
I lack
I miss

I lack

Do I breathe?
Can I breathe?
How do I breathe?
Do I want to…?

I am engulfed
I succumb
I dissolve
I fall
I melt
I sustain
I abandon
Do I abandon?
Am I abandoned?
Am I you?
Are you me?
Am I me?
Will me be?

Becoming
Transing
I suspend

Suspended
I sustain
I endure
I sigh
(I sigh)
I miss
I lack
I yearn

I ache
I kiss…air
I touch
Nothing
I doubt
I desire
I wait
Do I heal?
Wait?

Void
A void
Heal
No
Become
Trans the void

I am anxious
I lose
I am lost
Am I lost?
What have I lost?
I miss
I lack
I lose…patience

I am in abyss
I twitch I procrastinate
I drift
I change
Do I change?
What if I change?
Do you change?
A void

I distract

I shut down
(Sigh)
I fake

I hide
I waste…away
How long?
The bridge
To Trans
I sustain
I sustain
I am discomfort
I crave
I miss
I wait
I wait

Our external appearance is anything but our final form

LOVE AND OTHER THINGS (from the archives)

Nick Lawson

MY DARLING, MY LOVE, MY HEART

I am so very happy that I have found you!
Maybe I seem undecided but I assure you I am in this 110%
I am slightly anxious about it all…

The truth is, you are the one thing I am sure of in this world

MY DARLING

An unexpected but fateful meeting

How I have longed for you
How I have felt I may just die if I were to go another moment without you
Never have I met someone quite like you before

YOU ARE AMAZING!

The first time I laid eyes on you, I knew I could not even try to speak
Awkward fumbles, tripping over my tongue
Just staring from across the room, unable to look away
We made eye contact briefly

Before I could even try to say a word my legs had carried me away

VISIONS OF YOU

Taking off your work boots at my front door, you look up and see me.
I'm leaning against the wall, watching you with a smirk.
'I've been waiting for you!'
You eagerly rush over, scooping me up in a loving embrace.
As you carry me into the bedroom, kissing me, you throw me onto the bed. You can't keep your hands off me and I don't want you to stop.
Running your hand through my hair, you grab a fistful and pull me into your kiss. Your other hand has found its way into my pants. Indescribable waves of pleasure begin to flow through me.
Ohhhhhh, how I've dreamt of this day and now I'm at your mercy and you taste delicious!

I'M SORRY

It took me so long to realise that you and I are meant to be!

Seeing you standing there in your oversized shirt and boxers, just casually leaning against the wall, watching me, looking at me the way you do... You just drive me absolutely wild!

DO YOU HEAR ME WHEN I SAY

I love you!
I miss you more and more with each passing day!

I'M NOT LOOKING FOR

Shallow interactions or meaningless flings
I'd rather spend my hours alone; I have left that
self-serving life behind!

I COULD

Go back but that would be my own self-destruction

I WILL ALWAYS

- Love You
- Respect You
- Honour You

PLEASE FORGIVE

YOURSELF

We were just kids.
It wasn't your fault; you aren't to blame!
We did what we had to in order to survive.
We are adults now and it is safe to be who we are.

ME

I'm sorry, for the things I have done to hurt you!

PLEASE

I just want to come home to you.
Home to love, where I belong, safe with you.

Where the world falls away
in that space in between
in your heart
not far from your oh-so-kissable lips.

OH PLEASE

Won't you write yourself into my life?
I'm an open book with blank pages
Everything I do is for love, for you
I want to share my life with you on earth
Let's start over anew together

I PROMISE

Not to hurt you,
not to break your fragile heart
My heart is yours until the end of time

INFINITELY YOURS

For all time
I love you
ALWAYS

WE WILL

Live by the ocean
Walk hand in hand along the shore
Make love by the moon

WITH unwavering eye contact
Only us existing together

Your eyes, like an ocean
Bright like a summer's day
They cast light upon me
A glow that warms my entire being
You light the way
You are the sun to my moon
It is written in the stars

As I bask in your gloriousness
Swim in your presence
    The tide starts to come in
    Stirring up your once-calm seas
    Crashing waves of ecstasy engulf us
    I know you won't let me drown
    We float safely inside a pocket of love
    Higher and higher amongst the clouds
    Blissfully ascending into divine unity
Just infinitely being

    You and I
    One soul, our essence entwined
    Together forevermore; our bond can never be broken

WE WILL

- Change our ways
- Use public spaces for creative endeavours
- Find the lost souls of our realm
- Arm them with the tools to create good health
- Help them to build their own little paradise

* Nurse our Mother Earth back to health

* She will start to emit a beautiful frequency that reverberates all around her.

A vibration of happiness, joy and love will spread worldwide like a pandemic.

The plants and animals will begin to regenerate, repopulate and flourish.

The veil of fog will lift
After spending an eternity dreaming
The dead will awaken

THEY WILL

* Wonder how they managed to get so caught up in frivolous and unimportant things in their past lives.

* Realise the noise of the world deafened them to the call of their names.

* See they have been fighting a war that has long since been over.

* Return home, slowly at first, then with a forceful urgency, to their loved ones—the loved ones who had given up hope and imagined their demise.

* See life, everyone and everything is beautiful.

R KISSES

E LIFE, PULL M

ER IF ONLY

R JUST

ORE BREAT

DE L'ESPOIR POUR LES COMMUNAUTÉS LGBTIQ AFRICAINES
Hope for African LGBTIQ communities

Kashindi Shabani Gady

Maybe it's the name—Congo—which conjures up images of Africa before colonialism. In the name, the imagination sees and hears villagers beating drums, inviting all to dance under the moonlight.

Maybe the Congo reminds us of Patrice Lumumba, the one true leader of Africa who genuinely believed we deserved and could do better.

Or of these two things—the sweet potato and the small fish called *sambaza*, which are in Lake Kivu and the Ruzizi River.

Then, of course, there is the immortal Rumble-in-the-Jungle heavyweight fight between Muhammad Ali and George Foreman, and the shouts of 'Ali bomaye' that continue to echo through history from the stadium in Kinshasa where the fight took place in 1974.

I live in Bukavu, in the commune of Ibanda, in the Nyalukemba-Nguba district, in the Province of South Kivu, in the east of the Democratic Republic of Congo, in Central Africa. I am from a family of nine children, including seven boys and two girls and a son who died during the war of 1996. I am the second child, my father and my mother are farmers and our house is baked brick with three bedrooms.

Our LGBTQ community lives separately, in different municipalities and provinces, but we keep in touch by WhatsApp, email and our advocacy meetings.

Every Monday is briefing day with the Savie NGO team and some of our members. Tuesday is a field day and also for answering letters. Wednesday is for advocacy in public places—the market, schools, churches and other places where people gather—to speak on to speak on the LGBTIQ cause. Thursday is for the collation of various reports from Wednesday's field work. Friday is for the preparation of the next week, because Saturday is a half day. Finally, our work can resume online.

Our activities include WhatsApp group support; peer-to-peer training sessions; workshops; collecting data on persecution because of sexual orientation; HIV/AIDS clinic visits; support for refugees, asylum seekers and sex workers; informal financial skills training; work on accessing basic education; and advocacy. What I value most about my community is the love that exists between our members, seen in the mutual help between us in the search for work and emotional support during bereavements, marriages and times of difficulty.

The trans person is often associated with witchcraft and considered to be against nature—someone who does not have children or form a family, who does not have access to education, health. So a trans person's family must chase him/her from the house because the trans person is a source of curse—poverty, no blessing to God.

In 2018, during the persecution of the LGBTIQ community, I survived thanks to the external contact of an online newspaper *Gay Star News*. I was afraid of the police, the National Intelligence Agency (ANR) and the Directorate General of Immigration (DGM), the institutions working for the internal security of the Democratic Republic of Congo, because I am homosexual, and they are there to track people in my community.

It tends to be the case that LGBTIQ communities in sub-Saharan African countries are under attack. In country after country we are persecuted, discriminated against, harassed, beaten, jailed or subjected to 'corrective rape'. Our very lives are criminalised and threatened. In 34 out of 54 countries in Africa, laws are maintained that criminalise consensual sex between men and same-sex relations between adults, and 24 maintain laws that apply to women. In the Congo, persecution of the LGBTIQ community is getting worse due to a lack of laws and the benediction of churches, leadership and unhappy populations.

It is against this backdrop of hostility and violence that LGBTIQ communities struggle to survive: to claim their sexual orientation, gender identity and gender expression; secure their human rights and work environments; to live with dignity and without fear; and to address the scourge of HIV/AIDS.

The Democratic Republic of Congo is one of the poorest countries in the world, with a weak and underfunded health system that is in a fragile phase of reconstruction after decades of difficulties. Although the prevalence of HIV in the DRC decreased from 0.9% in 2016 to approximately 0.8% in 2017, certain groups continue to be disproportionally at risk of acquiring HIV. In 2017, the estimated HIV prevalence rate was 8.2% among men who have sex with men and 5.7% among sex workers.

Most African LGBTIQ organisations are engaged in one of the most urgent human rights struggles today. We work with tenacity and courage to combat discrimination and stigma, using the law and advocacy to claim our human rights. We deliver life-saving services from mobile HIV clinics to peer support groups, and care for HIV-positive members of the community.

We often have to use code numbers to identify clients and members, in order to protect ourselves from being identified and subjected to harassment, detainment or beatings. We store staff information (CVs, names and so on) offsite to preserve anonymity and security in case our offices are raided. But despite inadequate resources and real danger, indefatigable activists simply refuse to give up on the struggle for freedom and justice.

Patrice Lumumba wrote: 'The more closely united we are, the better we will resist oppression, corruption, and those divisive maneuvers which experts in the policy of "divide and rule" are resorting to.'[21]

---

[21] https://www.blackpast.org/global-african-history/1959-patrice-lumumba-african-unity-and-national-independence/

I learned the power of living by accepting myself. Being in my city means living where I can see friends, family and people I can ask for help and give help to. Our bodies are God's creation and should be protected.

We will keep fighting for our rights.

Savie Asbl NGO LGBT PGEL is a group of rural LGBTIQ internally displaced people and refugees in the Democratic Republic of Congo.

Website:

YouTube channel:

做你想做的人
Zuò nǐ xiǎng zuò de rén[22]

Tiff Tan and anonymous collaborators

Our scene is a cafe in Carlton. Three are gathered there. They are men, or something like it. They sit at a table outside, rugged up against the cold, the winter sun shining.

One is the hero, with a story to tell, one is a documentary filmmaker, and I am a friend along for the ride. The hero knows that people love the stories of asylum seekers. He is testing different points of intervention for his own story. He has already worked with many others to tell it. This is a fragment of the conversation that day.

Filmmaker: When did you know you were trapped in the wrong body?

Hero: When I was four, I was wearing a skirt. I was crying. I didn't want it. When I was five, everyone called me tomboy, my nickname. Maybe it's fun to them, but I don't like it.

Filmmaker: And how did that make you feel?

Hero: I feel sad, disappointed. You don't know who to talk to. Your parents aren't on your side. You don't think about it, you just forget it. I was a good person, always listening. I had no freedom; I cannot tell anyone. I don't want to hurt anyone.

Filmmaker: Who are you afraid of hurting?

---

[22] 'Be who you want to be': one friend's response to the hero's news of his transition.

Hero: We cannot say we don't want to hurt anyone—we cannot say that. I need to protect them.

Filmmaker: Who?

Hero: My family. In their heart, I'm still a girl. They have to pretend I'm still a girl.

Filmmaker: Do they know you've changed your body?

Hero: My mother asks, 'Why is your voice changing?'. I say, 'I'm sick, my voice is dry, not enough water'. My mother know, but she don't know.

Filmmaker: Do you pretend to make them happy?

Hero: It's not pretending because they forget everything. Nothing is in front of their eyes, so they are not unhappy.

Filmmaker: What's your relationship like with your family?

Hero: We are close. With my mother, I take her everywhere. I massage her body every night before she sleeps.

Filmmaker: Do you believe you will lose this good relationship with your mum if they know you are transgender?

Hero: That's why I can't go back. My mother is a superwoman. My brother was attacked by men with a knife when he was driving my mother. She caught the knife and held the blade in her hand to protect my brother. The blood was running down.

In our family, our mum is the queen; we all listen to her. Before she married, she was a public speaker. She was the eldest. She grew up in the war; she carried her brothers and sisters to safety on her back.

Mother's mouth is like a god. She says, if you change your gender, you won't go up, you'll go down. Buddhism teaches that.

Filmmaker: I haven't come across Buddhism that supports that kind of thinking.

Hero: You respect the body you have; that's what my mother says. I told her I want to change and she was crying, so I said fine. I wait a few years, then she forget, then I do it.

Filmmaker: One part of your mind believes what your mother said, another part of your mind—transitioned. How do those parts sit with each other?

Hero: I don't think too much; I just forget it.

Filmmaker: How is love experienced in your family?

Hero: Conditional love. You love your family. You love your body. You need to know how to play the role.

Filmmaker: When you came to Australia, when you got accepted to the school here, how did you feel?

Hero: I just did it. I didn't prepare. I was living with my brother in Singapore. He didn't know I was gone. Not for one month. He thought I was still in my room.

Filmmaker: Some of these questions inevitably will be hits and some of these will be misses. We are in a process of finding out what the story is really about and what is the best way to tell it. A complex and multidimensional process is unfolding, with many moving parts—the hero, the filmmaker and time.

Me: I'm struck by how the hero's 'I 'emerges in dialogues with others—the family, the mother, the filmmaker, the future audience—and is made up of multiple voices and viewpoints. His particular view is there in the way it pulls the questions and perspectives of others off course, even as he feels his way towards his truth.

Transgender people are subject to severe discrimination and criminalisation in Malaysia. Gender diversity once had a degree of acceptance, but shifts in national politics in the 1980s changed this situation. Nonetheless, a recent survey suggests majority support for transgender rights in Malaysia.[23]

> *We strongly urge the government to end its persecution of transgender people and LGBTI people at large. …It is high time that we Malaysians embraced our LGBTI friends, family, neighbours and co-workers, instead of allowing them to experience hate and condemnation.*

Preethi Bhardwaj, Amnesty International Malaysia
Interim Executive Director[24]

---

[23] See: https://williamsinstitute.law.ucla.edu/publications/opinion-trans-rights-malaysia/

[24] https://www.amnesty.my/2020/07/11/government-must-end-persecution-of-transgender-people/

Have you lived with yourself long enough to know who you are?

SUGAR INTO SYRUP

Finnley Stirling

Painting my lips black and pretending to enjoy
loud music that sounded like screaming began my
process of fading into
the background of what we understood
mainstream femininity to be.

I spent time settling
my blank space of a chest
into feeling everything deeply, resenting everything pink
and colouring my hair
every other day of the week.

But people don't notice girls in black
and I knew femininity needed to be flashy, loud,
I needed to sparkle.
So, I painted my nails 'Alaska Young' blue,
used my love of the classics and flowery words
to write myself into the kind of girl
you might write into a poem.

Who pulled you through blurred city lights
and thrust you headfirst into self-actualisation,
who showed you the stars or rising sun
in the frosty, final hours of the evening with
red cup and poetry collection in hand.

It was in darkness, under the covers of my single bed
once I'd wiped my eyes of colour and imagination,
unhooked my body from a glimmering nonchalance
and shut off the projection of a sunny disposition
that I learned what happens to the heroine once the lights go
down.

The stutter, the gasp of recognition
there is no way around, and
I knew I needed sunlight, instead of houselights.
So, I scrubbed away the blue from my fingertips,
warmed my chest with patience and forgiveness
until I was stripped of my usual
hiding places and
I felt my femininity slip.

They were left in her wake.
The beauty of my otherness
brimming to the surface.
I was the honey, golden and warm
transformed from the centre of flowers.
I am the evolution, the process of turning
sugar into syrup.

IN UNHEARD-OF PLACES

Hester J. Rook

hollow out your throat and sing for me, my love.

in this acid-burnt haze we

swell and touch and move against

the autumn breeze,

feel it whisper against your skin, feel it fling up the hairspray and glitter and

sequin-sheen of those around us.

smoke billows from the mouth of a blonde with a side-shave

and for a moment everyone is the most

beautiful person on this earth.

the light slants gold and pink and we are baptised with other people's sequins,

with lemon lime and bitters laced with vodka,

with the glimmer of sweat and kisses

yours and mine and those we find, glowing under UV or transformed daylight.

our uber driver parades the rainbow flag his kid drew in kindy,

a splash of coloured-pencil home across his dash.

he asks how to do their hair like mine, woven with carnations
blessed with two nights of joy.

the dance floor hymns to *make me feel*

and not even the man who claims your true name is drag

or the slip-dash beat of my fearful heart

can temper the upswell,

the healing, the in-draw of oxygen that means we can breathe

and breathe and breathe.

wind your fingers about my own, my love.

my carnations are strewn about my sheets, your skin is my own
and mine is yours

and we are flooded with so much holiness we could

open our ribs

and belove this world.

LIONS, TIGERS AND BEARS

Son Vivienne

When I was a teenager in the 1980s and early '90s, I had an unhealthy obsession with the Cowardly Lion from *The Wizard of Oz*. Like, not just a fan. I lived in a fantasy world. I imagined myself as a youthful Bert Lahr. When I grew up, I would get my big break and play his role in a remake. I found myself in the Emerald City, anonymous, ready to be remade, when I was 15. Now I am a wise old man, and I share this cautionary tale for naughty kids. It is unfinished, incomplete, and a bit sticky around the edges.

There was an incident behind our shed. At an average family barbecue. With my older brother's friend. I tried to tell my mum about it, but she was either too drunk to care or didn't really understand that peer-pressured pashing and non-consensual fingering was not okay.

I was tired of trying so hard to fit in. That night, I packed my schoolbag and caught a bus interstate. Nowadays the bus driver would ask questions. Now I would probably need evidence of a negative test result at boarding. I probably looked about 12, but I was clean and tidy, so I got away with it. I had the trappings of privilege, an old Canon SLR camera around my neck, everywhere I went. My favourite beanie was a hood with lion ears, a mane and woven wool plaits down either side. I could pull it down tight so only my nose and chin were exposed, my eyes veiled.

I have a treasure box of prints, still packed in their original yellow chemist-shop sleeves with their 35-millimetre negatives. The box is labelled, 'In event of fire, take these first'. There are some canisters that may or may not have been exposed. I can't afford to get them developed but they might contain memories, beyond the edges of my current mental range.

Now everything is in cloud storage to make sure we don't forget, but it's still hard to remember. The other day, I heard a parent arguing with their kid about whether they had the right to keep a sneaky shot they'd just taken on their phone 'for posterity'. The kid said the parent had to delete it, because they hadn't given consent. I felt sorry for them both.

When I first arrived in the city I gravitated towards the inner west. I remember sitting in a park, next to a long, white wall covered in excellent graffiti. I spent hours taking photos of it, and the dogs playing nearby.

Later I walked in the nearby cemetery, a bit daunted, trespasser of spirits. It was spooky and beautiful, with strands of setting sun filtered through enormous Moreton Bay figs, like ancient elders. I felt the presence of dead-buried-noisy-white-people. I tried to turn them down, to listen for older spirits. The original people, talking around fires, telling bedtime stories to adventurous children. I still listen to stranger-adults talking in lost languages as I drift off to sleep. Stoned in a cemetery, or headphones and meditation app, these are my tricks for feeling safer.

The night I left home. There was a fire in the half 60-gallon drum. And. So. Much. Beer. A constant stream of blokes in utes heading off to get more from the local drive-thru. Lumbering back in through the gates, carrying cases, like an ant-trail. Dad's dogs barking at their leery faces, distorted in the firelight.

In the big city, I photographed random people. I guess I wasn't threatening; my camera looked like a toy, so strangers would just chat. My lens was a protective filter between me and the real world. Down by the stagnant lake near the showgrounds I made friends with a homeless guy and his dog. When I left that share house, I took him some hot chips and a six-pack to share. I can't remember his dog's name now.

Later I met Tiger, and my whole world changed. I moved into her spare room because she needed someone to help pay the rent. She didn't say it or probably even know it, but she also needed help with her daughter, Dotty. She was eight, like my little sister, and I think she felt safe with me. We connected. Tiger trusted me to care for her. Tiger was working nights a lot, so it worked well.

Back then strange things happened, and I'm still not sure whether some stuff is real or imagined or a bit of both. One particular night plays in my dreams, like a home movie on loop. A David Lynch meets Brian De Palma mash-up, definitely directed by a pale, stale male.

We were in a club with soft blue light and really loud, deep bass. It was a warehouse with cavernous ceilings, and there were heavy-duty power cables hanging down to industrial machines. In place of engines there were digital screens, morphing time and space. People were plugging themselves in through some concealed port in their bodies, so that they could connect with one another. There was dancing, but not to any particular kind of music, just beats.

Bodies moved in fabulous, elaborate contortions. They were amazing. Tattoos and glitter and leather harnesses and eye make-up that made them all look like magical beasts. I was wearing my lion beanie—and I met an actual bear! He had a thick beard and a hard, round tummy covered in a furry pelt that flirted through his vest. He looked after me. The drinks were potent, and I remember their impact as if it was being delivered straight into my veins, or through one of the power cables. There were luminescent jelly shots too. I can't remember how the evening ended. I think maybe there was a raid, because in my dreams I sometimes see blue and red flashing lights.

I'm glad that I couldn't see the future back then. Even though it might have made things different between Tiger and I, it would have blown my tiny little mind to know that my nubile midriff could grow its own fur.

Another vignette. I'm pushing Dotty on a swing. She's really too old for it, but she loves it, the feeling of flight. It was a windy day and Tiger was watching, looking kind of sad. Mother and daughter with long hair blowing in every direction, blue and pink streaks. We were all pleased (and surprised) by the outcome of my home hair salon. Maybe we had matching nail polish? Dotty was screaming and laughing and begging Tiger to hop on the other swing. Tiger was resisting, but there was a glimmer in her eye. Eventually Tiger gave in, and I pushed them both, taking turns. I could feel the tight muscles and skin stretching over Tiger's scapulae and the warm, soft padding over Dotty's kidneys.

I hoped my touch felt okay, strong and assured but not invasive. And suddenly I flashed back to his cold hands slipping under the back of my jumper, stroking my lower back and circling forwards, around the top of my jeans.

When I snapped back into my body, Dotty was slowing herself down on the swing, and Tiger was standing bent over, holding onto the iron frame to stabilise herself. I realised she'd just thrown up. We both rushed over, Dotty in the lead, a small mama bear taking charge. Tiger looked up and smiled weakly, asked me for the water bottle. She said it was motion sickness. Dotty held her hand and murmured to her, inane kid things in a low voice, all the way home.

I think things started going bad when Tiger brought Guard West home. But oh my god, he was hot! Blonde and muscly, strong but a bit fey—like an older, beefier version of Daniel Johns. He was charming, and we all fell in love with him. He made the best spinach-and-fetta gozleme, perfect healthy snack food for movie nights.

I made friends with an artist, Glenda, who lived up the street. She was probably only ten years older than me, and she had a missing tooth. She said people thought she was 'a druggy' because of the gap and because she was Aboriginal. She had wisdom. Like wrinkles, broken teeth deserve respect when you've earned your stripes in the battles of life.

She didn't like Guard West, but she never told me why. And I could never explain why we called him that, always both words like they were one name. Because he wasn't an asshole; he just had a calm authority that made you defer to him without question and go along with any idea.

Glenda's art was stunning and shocking. She taught me how to skin roadkill and dry out the bits that were good for sculpture and weaving. We stole road signs together. Our favourite was a bright yellow one that read 'NO ACCESS PERMITTED'. She spray-painted 'stolen land' on it, and it won heaps of art awards. I taught her how to dehydrate kombucha scobies, and we experimented with stitching them together to make garments. We never quite got the balance of strength and fragility right, but their translucence and texture were beguiling. White collectors loved them. We loved the acronym; something so nerdy about 'selective combination of bacteria and yeast'. Scobies are a kind of benevolent alien life form, less bloody and better for your gut than roadkill.

The first time I slept with Tiger, it was with Guard West too. It's a little blurry, which is kind of funny because Guard West suggested documenting our tryst on my daggy old camera. Pre selfies and sex tapes, it was an illicit and appealing idea. The images would have been beautiful—because, in retrospect, we were. Those blurs, our bodies traced over one another, might be captured within one of the undeveloped film canisters. It would be hard to see we three together again, but I'd like to remember more clearly.

They made me feel sexy. It was the first time I really connected with my body. I'd just had my hair clipped with a number two, and I felt alien to myself. I had been thinking about starting testosterone but wasn't really sure. Guard West leaned back on the bedhead. I felt vulnerable spread-eagled on my back, like one of Angel's possums about to be skinned. Guard West cradled my head between his legs stroking my bristles like a cat, and I felt reassured. Tiger was so gentle and kept checking in, asking if I was okay. I'd never felt so attended to, so loved. They showed me ways that I never imagined my body could feel.

I'm not sure that I'll ever feel quite that wonder—complete awe—again. Perhaps it's a first-time thing. When I watched them later, fucking somewhat more conventionally, they were also a bit silly, making up names for yoga poses that were variants on downward dog, cat, and cow... Something clicked and I realised that sex can be fun. I miss that. I miss them. Before things got bad, we were a happy little posse, an unconventional family.

One time we were all at a music festival. It was one of those 'reclaim the streets' events with the main road closed to traffic. Tiger was scheduled for mid-afternoon on one of the smaller stages. There were some delays because the equipment was late arriving, so she got to perform during magic hour. I've definitely got photos of this, because I remember the light was similar to when I first arrived in the city, in the cemetery. The stage was shadowed by fig trees, and Tiger was backlit and golden.

It seems weird to save up pension money to get rolls of film developed and digitised. But I wonder if Tiger's transcendence in my memories has survived on celluloid.

She covered Peggy Lee's 1958 version of 'Fever'. It was perfect–velvety, vulnerable, sexy and strong. The crowd were enchanted. It was a complete change of mood to the doof we'd been dancing to, but she pulled it off. She hadn't said anything about the preparation, but the logistics must have been tricky. Some of her music-school mates materialised with their instruments. Snare drum, double bass and bass guitar. She led them on stage as if she was seducing a harem of willing nubiles...and their notes swirled around her, with tangible texture.

We stood and swayed, Guard West's body spooning mine, and mine spooning Dotty's. Someone in front of us had a joint, and as the sun lit the smoke I remember thinking, 'That's what love must look like'. 'Fever, till you sizzle... What a lovely way to burn.'

No one from before knew where I lived, so it was hard for my mum to find me. We didn't have mobile phones or email addresses back then. I ran into someone from school on King Street. They said they nearly didn't recognise me. I blushed when they said my old name, so they knew it was me. They told me that Mum had had an accident. That she was desperate to know whether I was dead or alive. I thought that was a little dramatic. To be honest, I hadn't really thought about 'the before' that much.

I rang home from a public phone. My brother answered and I hung up almost before I heard his voice, as soon as I heard the coins drop. I walked around for a while, my heart racing. I took some photos of graffiti and flowers to calm down. Now that I knew, I couldn't get an image of Mum's broken leg out of my head. Eventually I rang back, using another 40 cents, warm and sweaty from clutching. I only had a dollar, so we got cut off before she finished speaking, but already she'd niggled me into going back. I promised Dotty it was just for a visit and that I'd be back before she knew it.

Long story short: it was as if I'd never left. Mum loved being helplessly reclined on the lounge. Bossing us all around, a mix of regal and whiny. She was vague about how the accident had happened, which made me think it wasn't as simple as tripping down the stairs. My dad was noticeably silent on the subject and magically disappeared whenever it came up. I started wearing my lion beanie again, which was good because it hid my short hair and stopped people staring.

Once I tried to talk to Mum about why I'd left and what I'd learned about myself since. She laughed and said that we all did stupid things when we were kids. Not to worry about it. My brother straight-up avoided me.

Mum liked to keep me captive when she was bored or needed affection. She had me pinned on the lounge with her cast, watching some tedious game show. My brother brought her a cup of tea and glared at me. I looked away and waited for him to leave. He kept staring until I blushed. Mum stared at him—three points in a triangle—and finally he spat it out. He wanted to know if I was a 'fucking fag'. The canned audience laughter filled the silence, and the host sang out, 'Noleen Rice, come on down!'.

I denied it. They didn't accept the truth of my past, and I didn't want them to have a piece of my future.

Those realities pierced me like icy shards, dredging up my other life and the things I'd been pressing down. That night

I summoned my Cowardly Lion and slipped away quietly into the darkness.

When I got back everything was different. Tiger's mum was visiting and staying in the spare room that had been mine. Sometimes I thought she was the wicked witch. When the witch was around, Tiger melted into the floorboards and Dotty stopped listening. I tried to stand up for them, but I was weak. Guard West was using way too much, and not around very much. I made a tiny spot in the corner of the lounge and tried to make myself invisible while the tornadoes whirled around me.

There is no real end to this story. What actually happened was tragic and unfair, and I'm still carrying it in a locked-away space inside. I'm not really up for sharing that stuff right now. It might seem abrupt and inadequate, but the only thing I've learned is the yellow brick road is not linear. It might start in a vortex when you're a little person in munchkin land, but there is no destination. The Emerald City could be any new place where you find yourself a stranger. There are no magical ruby slippers or hot air balloons to take you there. It's true that 'There's no place like home', but sometimes that's the problem.

CORPOREAL

Shreya Tekumalla

Phase one—creation

A gust of fresh oxygen swirls around his lungs, and he awakens to find himself in the middle of a city street.

One foot in front of the other. It's muscle memory—he weaves through the lanes with a practised gait.

He can feel the sun on the top of his head, softened by the cool breeze tumbling across the sidewalk. His shoelace gets caught on a crack in the pavement and he's yanked backwards, nearly losing his balance before he catches himself. Sliding the strap of his backpack back onto his shoulder, he feels the edge of it dig into his skin through his jacket, and he feels warm.

He feels every single one of his footfalls against the pavement. Step by step. It's a rhythm. A heartbeat. He's here. He's alive.

As he passes by shopfronts with their glaring glass windows, he catches glimpses of himself in the reflective surfaces. A round face peers back at him every so often. Small glimpses, small shards of awareness stitch themselves back together to reveal a person—here to remind him that every second of this existence here is stolen from someone else.

He forces his gaze away from the makeshift mirror and tucks his hands into his pockets. The inside of his denim jacket is worn and rough.

Rough.

He grips his fists and feels the edge of his knuckles bite into the coarse fabric. His hands are rough.

Analysing the pavement, he sidesteps a lamppost and skids against a spot of wet mud. He begins to wrench back control and slowly, steadily, he can feel the weight of his feet in his shoes again. As the sun begins to set over the edge of a skyscraper, bathed in its beam of light, feeling begins to return to his limbs.

Another side street. Another pedestrian crossing. Another shopfront and he's swept up into a crowd without any warning—he's reached the heart of the city. Surrounded by a sea of strangers, he lets the buzzing fill his skull and breathes a sigh of relief.

Passing through the business district, looking out onto the street and carefully avoiding the glass storefronts, he feels the hackles rise on the back of his neck as he becomes aware of a pair of eyes that keep looking at him.

He eventually realises that they belong to a young lady walking just a few paces ahead of him. For a moment, he sees himself in her eyes. Mop of short hair. A silhouette covered by a large coat. Heavy footfalls. Her wary eyes discreetly flicker back and forth.

Quickly, he ducks his head and lengthens his stride for long enough to pass in front of her, giving her some breathing room. It's what a decent man should do to assuage her worry—make her feel safer.

People continue to pass by him on the street, their eyes sliding over him and onto the next thing. He steals those gazes for himself. As he walks, he retreats into his mind, where he slows those moments down and replays them. The middle-aged man who he nearly bumped into saw flashes of a denim jacket. The businessperson talking on the phone got a glimpse of his muddy black sneakers. The woman who walked out of the shop reflexively turned in his direction when he raised his hand to push his glasses further up on his nose.

Person to person. Moment to moment. Tossed between them like a boat on rough seas.

Their worlds dance together for moments and then separate. His existence in their life is so fleeting that, for all they know, he's always been here.

Stars are born over millions of years, but he's found a way to create and destroy universes within seconds—and his place in every single one of them belongs to him.

Phase two—preservation

The train doors pry themselves open with a screech, and he tilts his head towards them just in time to watch a man with impressive facial hair walk into the carriage.

Perched in a window seat a few rows away, his eyes follow the stranger as he paces towards an empty seat and settles himself into it.

Does he even feel lucky?, he wonders.

He detaches his nails from the inside of his palm and runs a finger along the underside of his chin. The hairs there are soft. Delicate. Like spun sugar—they would dissolve with the smallest drop of water. For a second, he allows himself to imagine them as longer, coarser, rough against his hand when he strokes his jaw. Then, without opening his eyes, he closes his fist around that reality and feels it shatter.

With a beleaguered groan, the train heaves slightly before beginning to pull away from the station. As the clinking of the wheels on the track speeds up and becomes a pervasive humming, he lets his palm fall open and feels the embers grip onto his skin for a moment before being pulled away by the wind.

Eyes still closed, his penance is aided by the sounds thrown out by the gears of life churning around him. Suddenly, the trains banks left, and he's shocked awake when his head is thrown against the window. It takes a moment for his vision to adjust to the overhead lights, and he blearily notices a face peering at him.

A kid. Well…maybe. She looks about his age. Her gaze has snapped towards him at the sound of his skull thudding against the glass, but her movement follows through into her taking a glance at the rolling landscapes. Then, just as quickly as she looked up, she crosses one leg over the other and returns her attention to her phone.

He averts his eyes as well. Turning to the window, he lets his vision go unfocused and replays her gaze over and over again. Reverses it. Slows it down. He breaks down the moments, splits them from each other and weaves them together again.

In the film that plays back, he observes himself from her perspective. Just a stranger. A random kid about her age. Slightly dishevelled. Shoulders slouched, braced against the seat to keep his head from lolling forward. Legs spread, feet pointing outwards.

Hands buried somewhere in the massive expanse of a denim jacket. He was already here when she sat down. To her, he's always been here. He'll always be here.

He allows himself to stay here—frozen in her gaze—just a little bit longer.

When the train rolls past some supermarkets, he shakes himself out of his stupor and realises the rest of the carriage is empty. Makes sense—his stop is one of the last on the line.

He fishes his phone out of his pocket and goes to check the time, but he's distracted by the pair of eyes that are reflected back at him in the black screen. A beat passes and they blink once. Twice. Completely expressionless.

He tries to unravel what they see, find himself in them, but it's not a face that wants to know him. They just want him to relinquish his place in their world.

The sparks—embers from a broken universe—dance in the sliver of moonlight that has stolen its way into the carriage before they fade away, taking the heat from his fingertips with them.

Phase three—destruction

The sole of his shoe disappears under the surface of the puddle and the water is quick to creep up into his sock before he manages to yank his foot back. With a sigh, he steps around the puddle and squelches off into the carpark.

A light drizzle has descended. The streams of water sneak through slivers into the ever-slight depression in the worn concrete, and he can see them wind their way down car windshields. They refract the light thrown out by the street lamp, and it feels like blinking, glassy eyes surround him.

He pulls his collar more firmly up onto his neck.

Towards the back of the car park, near the gate by the supermarket, lurks a small, blue car almost completely disguised by the shadows. Without the two blinding headlights puncturing the darkness, there is nothing to betray that there is anything there at all.

By the time he makes it to the driver's side door, he has noticed the silhouette of his mother behind the rain-splattered window. She's facing the other direction, gesticulating wildly—

probably on the phone—and doesn't see him standing right next to her.

He sharply taps on the glass and his mother startles so violently that she drops her phone. When she notices him laughing at her, she rolls down the window and rolls her eyes good-naturedly.

'How was your day?' she mouths, reaching for the phone down where it has fallen.

He gives her two thumbs up in response and waves in the direction of the car floor. *Finish your call.*

By the time he's walked around to the other side of the car, she's hurriedly wrapping up the conversation with the person on the other end.

'Yeah, I'm at the train station right now. Mmm-hm. No, it's okay. It was my daughter—I'm picking her up. Okay. Okay, no problem, I'll get those papers to you by tomorrow and call you back—'

The rain has begun to pick up now. As the droplets hit his skin and roll off, they take pieces of him with them.

He doesn't realise that he has turned around to face the train platform until he hears a whirring behind him. He turns around to see his mother patiently gazing at him over the top of the lowered window.

He looks into her eyes. Eyes that he's all too familiar with—the ones she gave him. He doesn't know why he's hoping for anything different, but he just confirms what he already knows: she's looking at her beloved daughter.

'Ready to go?' she asks.

He lifts his head towards the sky, inhales deeply, and exhales. 'Yeah.'

He watches the mist formed by his breath swirl through the air for a moment before the droplets are carried away by the cool breeze that sweeps through the car park.

Smiling to himself, he lets his eyes fall shut, and the last thing he feels is the raindrops on his eyelids before he disappears into the darkness.

WORKING LATE

Jules Joy

Zef was working late again.

Anyone who had worked at the gallery knew she spent more time there than at home. To her these stark, white walls and the art on display had become her life. If she was being honest with herself, this place felt more like home than any place had.

Colleagues and co-workers would ask her about her life outside the gallery: did she have a partner, pets, hobbies? She came up blank.

'What do you do for fun?'

Fun. She almost laughed the word out. It came out short, sharp and a little too hard. What do you need fun for when you have purpose? They didn't understand.

Looking past her computer, from the window of the centre office she could see the entire gallery with a glance. It was strange how different the place looked without people, still beautiful but somehow hollow.

Usually Zef would pick up movement from the corners of her eyes throughout the day, some long-forgotten survival mechanism her eyes retained from a time when every movement was a threat, a danger. Frustrating when you are trying to focus, trying to work, but the eyes don't know they're part of a whole, they only know their purpose.

It must have become habit, because even tonight she could not keep her eyes from darting about, scanning the main gallery floor for movement that couldn't be there.

The exhibition stood empty. The gallery was never really dark; even at night it was bathed in a cool, colourless light made by small, cylindrical fixtures that hung above each piece, on display for an audience of no-one. A place like this was made to be viewed; the art, the walls, the gallery demanded it. Look. See.

From the outside the gallery stood, a tall, stark, white block of modernist curves and angles, its large, round windows like oversized portholes casting light into the seemingly lifeless landscape.

Even from the interior the light from the window that dominated the wall opposite the main exhibition illuminated the street; the pale light transformed the familiar sidewalk into something far more alien. The mismatch of brick and modern cement that made up most of the city replaced by smooth, angular tiles. A landing pad as alien as the building that stood on it.

If it wasn't for the lines joining the oversized windowpanes, it would almost seem as if there was nothing separating the well-heated room from the cold luminescence of the outside world.

For a moment Zef could feel it. A coldness spread through her body as a realisation began to take hold. For a moment she knew.

Zef shivered involuntarily, causing herself to look away.

What was she doing? She looked back to her work. Fifteen new expressions of interest in the last hour; they kept pouring in faster than she could read them. None of them quite right. None of them perfect. *It has to be perfect. People need to come; they need to see.*

Another shiver. The heating system playing up again. Nothing a hot cup of coffee wouldn't solve. Sighing, she found herself wishing yet again that they had a kitchen at office level.

Normally the walk down the main staircase was a highlight of her day; the sharp, angular metal gave a view of the building like no other as it followed the window line to the ground.

Not tonight. Tonight, she couldn't quite bear to be so exposed; the main gallery floor stood a chasm, the artwork looked right at her, and the window… She felt exposed. Vulnerable.

What is wrong with me?

Overtired and overworked. Instinctually she stuck close to the dividing wall that separated the ground floor kitchen from the gallery. The winding hallways and side rooms lit up as she passed, sensor lights another move towards their 'green initiative' and a lower power bill.

To those unfamiliar with it the small kitchen was disorientating; the chic black drawers and cabinets had been designed to blend in with the panels of the wall. They were right there in front of you, but if you didn't realise, you couldn't see them. New hires would complain about the design: 'Choosing style over practicality,' they would say.

If you're going to be something, you have to be it entirely, and this place didn't have a practical bone in its body. It was a gallery, even when it was a kitchen. *That's why it needs me.*

Zef of course could make a coffee here with her eyes closed, the place an extension of herself. There was no telling where her limbs ended and the kitchen began.

Her hand hesitated over the coffee: was caffeine a good idea? She was jittery enough. There was an assortment of teas that someone must have brought in but no-one ever seemed to drink.

Throwing one of the triangular tea bags into her mug, she flicked on the boiler tap… Nothing. Again. Nothing.

Shit. Looking in cupboard after cupboard, pretending she didn't already know where the kettle was, opening every drawer as if there was a chance it would appear. A performance for an audience of no-one. *If you're going to be something, you have to be it entirely.*

Zef knew. She could see the kettle in the boardroom as if it was right in front of her. The boardroom that was across the main gallery. That coldness again, rising.

Zef left the kitchen, slowly walking out from behind the dividing wall; each step felt like she was sinking. She felt eyes. *There is no-one here.* If thoughts are spoken in the mind, then this one was screamed. Drowning out the rest, the faint noise that she was so trying not to hear.

Be strong, keep moving. She didn't feel strong, she felt afraid. *This is silly.* She was getting that kettle! Eyes to the floor, she walked through the exhibition; she couldn't see movement out of the corners of her eyes. The creaking was the floorboards under her, not the walls closing in.

The dark hallway should have seemed foreboding, but it wasn't, it was sanctuary. The sensor lights sprang on, illuminating her path; the door to the boardroom stood open. They had used the meeting rooms as temporary storage for one of the smaller exhibits; paintings stood stacked in each corner.

Oil paintings of city streets, the buildings warped like they had been left out in the sun. Lonely, empty streets. On the middle of the table the kettle. Zef rushed to it, grasping it with both hands, careful not to look out the window. Not sure why. *What the hell am I doing!?*

Her eyes had been focused on the table. For a split second she thought she saw something; she thought she saw. No. *It's nothing.* She turned away. That's when she heard it, city streets, muffled but unmistakable.

No. She was in a meeting room. That was where she was. Not on the lip of a warped street, the noise growing louder. Her hands grasped the kettle, they did not angle off and twist like the buildings around her. She was not slowly beginning to warp; she couldn't feel her bones as they were moulded like clay.

She was in a room.

And she was stepping out of it.

She stood in the hallway. She did not look back as she crossed the hall and headed back towards the kitchen.

She was back in charge. Nothing had happened and she was fine. She walked across the gallery, her footsteps echoing across the empty space. She refused to notice as the walls of the exhibition turned to face her. Ignored the sound that rang in her head, the sound she did not hear. A thousand voices that spoke together, some so familiar. Look. See.

She walked faster to escape these things she did not notice. She locked eyes with the kitchen; she saw only the kitchen, which seemed to extend further and further away.

She walked swiftly towards it; she did not run. Even as she walked so fast that both feet were off the ground, so fast that she flung off her shoes onto the gallery floor, she was not running. Until finally she crossed the threshold of the kitchen doorway.

Looking down, her shoes sat on the ground in front of her, right where she had left them. In the centre of the gallery floor. *No. How?* She did not need to look up to know what was there, but she did anyway.

Past the exhibit, the window looked outside. Except there was no outside. Beyond the threshold of the window there was no street, just an endless sprawl of cool, colourless light and white walls.

Her mind desperately grasped at reason, a switch in the dark that could end the nightmare, but she could not find it, she could not stop looking.

She tried to focus on those lines that separated the windowpanes, the ones that didn't seem to be there. She wanted to close her eyes and focus on the feeling of her body in the room, to focus on safety, but she was too afraid to so much as blink.

She knew what was out there, was in here, in her. She knew. She looked right into its eyes. She saw and had been seen; her eyes grew big, wide with terror. The eyes were not there. She told herself. They did not cover the walls like pox, walls that were not thumping with a rhythm she desperately needed to ignore. She opened her mouth to scream, but she didn't hear anything. The only sound was that rhythm she could no longer pretend wasn't a beating, wasn't an unmistakable pulse.

A single thought echoed inside her.

Zef returned to her office, to her inbox. Twenty-five new expressions of interest; they kept pouring in faster than she could read them. None of them quite right. None of them perfect. *It has to be perfect. People need to come; they need to see.*

More eyes, a gallery needs eyes.

Safety in solitude, choice and being alone, waiting with the music—it keeps me alive

RE-EMERGENCE

Mohammad Taha

I woke every day the same way. I leapt out of bed with my eyes closed, then I opened my eyes. I kept my eyes closed and I leapt as an act of freedom. To have the certainty of safety is to leap without worry. I would leap, have my coffee and before I went to bed I ignited the kerosene lantern. I dreamt of a day when the sea would bring me a friend to drink coffee with and sleep in my spare room. Unfortunately, in all my time here no-one came knocking. Over time I learned to find love and sanctuary without measure within the darkness of my own heart, my own eyelids, my own room and my own lighthouse. The life in my lighthouse was a simple life, full of solitude and little hardships that made me feel so alive. Like the days when I didn't catch enough fish to take to the market, or the way the townspeople reacted to my dark complexion or my feminine sensibilities while having a body that appears to resemble the lighthouse from which I emerged every day. Their dismay never bothered me, because I lived within my heart, my eyelids, my room and my lighthouse. Within my life there was only safe harbour from the tumultuous waves that do not relent. But I also never forgave them for their hate and whispers. This was another act of freedom. They controlled their words, their occasional violence and how much they paid for my daily catch.

However, they could not control my forgiveness. I thought about forgiveness and letting go when I was cast out from my home as a child and travelled the land to find my place in the world; I felt unsafe so I sought out a safe place. For years I thought about forgiveness and how passive it is; I thought about how it left the parts of you that were fractured and healed without a history, triumphant or otherwise. I woke up on the 21st of the month of emerging, uMfumfu, the same way I always did: in my sanctuary, in safety and with my eyes closed. I poured my black coffee in my only cup and watched the clouds to see if I could go into the sea that day. Sunlight threaded the clouds with marvellous patches of hues. I was transfixed by the grace of heavens and started humming a lullaby my mother would hum for me as we stood in the kitchen of my childhood home as she taught me about the clouds and how they came to be; Gods of thunder and punishment, Gods of justice and mercy, about how thunder made ozone for the heavens and fertiliser for the earth. I hummed that lullaby, mesmerised by patterns of light. My thoughts, hums and wet cheeks were interrupted by thunder and rain. On the 21st of uMfumfu the rain started, and on the 21st of the month of scattering, uNhlangulanan, I decided that I was going to let my soul join my ancestors. I also stopped igniting the lantern, because I knew no-one was coming for me and it was time to stop waiting for company; time to truly make peace with the way things were, not what I wanted them to be. I wanted to scatter into the world and be a part of this cloud and this rain.

After eight months of rain and being locked in this lighthouse there was very little food, and the townspeople only looked after their own. I always knew that I wasn't one of them, but I had always wanted the secret convictions in my heart to be well-constructed falsehoods. As my food supply depleted, my waking changed. I no longer awoke with my eyes closed. Every morning I opened my eyes and I looked at the ceiling, paralysed by loss past, present and future. I made my peace with loss past long ago, but since the rain started, my solitude was no longer a matter of my choosing and freedom was the one luxury I could not part with. So, on the 21st of uNhlangulanan I decided it would truly be the month when I transcended my mortal flesh and with it the worry of rooms and lighthouses. After all of my journeying I deserved to keep my liberty and a new beginning. As days passed, I knew I had made the right decision. There was nothing here for me but grief. I started cleaning the lighthouse so that someone might find solace here when I was gone, like I once did after the one who left before me.

In my search I found an old grey radio, like the one my grandmother used to have. She used to turn it on the moment she woke up every day, and she would sit in the living room drinking tea and waiting. I used to think that she was wasting away by not leaving the house; I never knew why she listened to that radio all day. To my surprise the old radio was operational. I skipped over the news and the weather warnings because it was nothing I did not see outside my window or in town. Then I heard a song that I hadn't heard since I was a child. Whenever my grandmother would hear certain songs she would summon whatever strength she had and dance, and if I was nearby she would drag me and force me to dance with her. 'Sweet boy, come dance,' she would say. 'These are the songs of our people.' This time when I heard the song, I felt life. Not my own, but the lives of my people in words and rhythm. Slowly I felt my own life returning. In that moment, I knew why my grandmother turned on the radio every day and waited. She was not wasting away. She was trying to stay alive, and just like all of our people she knew how. A life insular was just a single life, but we learned how to transform music to save us in the darkest of times. When the music stopped, my heart was full of gratitude for my grandmother and for our people. The rain didn't stop, but every day I began to turn on the radio like my grandmother used to do. I drank coffee, found food some days, danced, and ignited the lantern every day. I still couldn't leap with my eyes closed because I didn't feel my freedom like I used to, but I knew that if I waited for a little while, I could hear the music of my people. Music that gave me a multitude of lives that I could borrow for a little while until I found my own. On the 30th of uNhlangulanan, I decided that I would wait for a little while, while I continued to listen to the music of my people, dance and look after the lighthouse. Music was sunlight filling the gloom of the clouds with life and beauty, reminding me that on the other side of the storm the light remains. Maybe by the next uMfumfu I will re-emerge.

ETHEREAL RELEASE FROM FORM

Madison Moffat

I was three, still openly wanting Mummy, but also seeking my own space. I had taken to sheltering in a large cardboard box in the lounge room, closing the flaps above me. Darkness, my breath, slight rustling whenever I moved. And Mummy's music.

These micro-memories include a self-removal from bodily determinism. Box open: light and embodiment. Box closed: solitude, tunes and an ethereal release from form. The boy's physique disappears, my spectre immersed in her true Cilla-Dione-Dusty-Diana voice. Each bodily evasion brought truth, yet male embodiment was the conduit through which I could be in the world of Mummy's love.

POP! I would leap up, box flaps bursting aside. Mummy would feign surprise with raised eyes, highlighting her divine sky-blue eye shadow. Giggling and gorgeousness. Lovingly reassured, I would sit back down, closing the flaps again.

Forty-eight years later, tracks like Dionne Warwick's 'Anyone Who Had a Heart' or Cilla Black's 'You're My World' invariably lead to a gentle tearing-up; I feel totally lost to them. These voices are burnt into my synapses, formative of my obsession with popular music in childhood and adolescence. Integral to my mental presence.

At five, I would turn to Mummy's late-teen brothers and request the needle be placed again on Suzi Quatro's '48 Crash'. They did it for the spectacle that would follow.

The echoing clap and thump would cue my stomping and the first riff, the dramatic strumming of my low-slung toy banjo. Suzi and I rockin' away together, simpatico.

Our new street was a sequence of white and pastel fibro. I was big now, starting kindergarten in the new year; so, allowed to cross our fenceless border and enthral in the company of The Three Girls. I would be doted on or, better still, sometimes just quietly coexist, the 'Girls room' becoming my space also.

1970s suburban kids invariably had long hair, but my curls and cowlicks were to die for. Just like Noosha, the lead singer of Fox, whose hit, 'S-S-S-Single Bed', was all over the radio. The Girls would coach me as I practised my Noosha. Giggling and gorgeousness. Significance was placed on emulating her luscious, vampish tones. Distinct praise was lavished on my honeyed sigh.

This sororal warmth was thwarted when Mummy conveyed her disapproval at finding her little Temptress draped in beads and bangles, my arms serpentine to the music. The annoyance was probably more towards the other girls, but I acknowledged it. An element of my self that was best discouraged had been unwittingly incanted. While I do not recall being told why, these visits did cease, and it was my fault.

'Harden My Heart' by Quarterflash is a manifesto for emotional atrophy. Its conclusion invites a repeated chant of a general denial of vulnerability; to fade. Still and silent, playing my tape of it from the radio, I would inwardly chant as invited. Solitude, tunes and an increasing dissonance with my changing bodily form. At 14, any playful gender dissension was now replaced with panic.

Karen had joked that hanging with me was like being with one of her female friends. Without (outward) jealousy, I would gently kiss, stroke and dote upon her and our mutual girlfriend. 'Isn't he such a lovely boy?' 'Yes, a real gentleman!' Giggling and gorgeousness.

We would sit, surrounded by my copies of *Smash Hits*, *Countdown* and *No. 1*, listening to one of my tapes. 'Harden My Heart' came on. Next thing I knew, Karen was snapping me out of a daydream, asking if I was okay. Where had my mind just gone? Flushed, I fumbled, mumbled and pointed to the cassette player. She reached her hand out to my arm. 'You're SO sweet!'

I knew Sigue Sigue Sputnik was my new favourite band before I heard a single note—upon viewing the two-page picture spread in *Smash Hits*. Their unapologetic gender fluidity gave me butterflies. The writer passed it off as hyper-styled outlandishness. Martin Degville, the lead singer, retorted: 'The higher the hair, the higher the heel, the higher the income.'

One 12-inch showed three stilettoed transgender women in lingerie and bondage gear, bearing whips and erections. Still having the power to give me a full chest and dewy eyes, the promotional video for '21st Century Boy' portrayed a world where the ultimate ticket to success is shameless self-expression. Variance as a delight. Giggling and gorgeousness.

When asked by a schoolfriend (later my best man) which Sputnik I most wanted to be like, I hesitated and said, Tony James.

I can't confess that it's Yana. To be her! Or just to be with her. With her and Tony. Her devastating smile, giggling 'Good girl!' as she strokes my face and kisses my forehead. Tony panting on my nape with each thrust.

It had been a few years since I had bought the 12-inch single of Boy George's 'No Clause 28'[25]. At 18, my preferred reading favoured hedonism over activism, so I had heard little else about this destructive UK law. When the local TV news service featured a protest against it, my demeanour betrayed my interest.

She raised her voice: 'If any of you boys turn out to be gay, you know where the front door is!' *Oh, Mother! Why the pretence that this was directed to all three of us?*

The panic attacks returned, only weeks after having been discharged. I had returned to the family home, until I got back on my feet. However, 'home' was the problem at hand. The anxiety mercifully subsided once I returned to self-exile, into my own abode.

> *There was just this overall, um, attitude that I took, and I even intellectualised it at one point—which I am wont to do.*

---

[25] 'Clause 28' refers to a series of laws under the UK's *Local Government Act 1988* that prohibited the 'promotion' of homosexuality, including as part of curricula within government schools.

And I remember thinking to myself in my bedroom: 'You know, I don't know what it is about me in particular. But it's there, and I'm HATED for it. And I'm going to hate the world back.

Madison Moffat interviewed by Greer McGeary,
Bent TV, 10 June 2022.

Stillness kept prompting a daunting self-connectedness. Pacing the bedsit walls was folly, so I took to pacing Newtown's streets instead. I often chose one particular tape to blast my ears to because of the bemusing pertinence of track 3, Alien Sex Fiend's 'Do You Sleep?'.

Nik Fiend's astringent humour, the repetitive beat and my matching strides served to moderate a different sleep-depriving surge from within; a plaguing unease, a near heartbreak. How can my body not be mine? What can such a thought even mean? Why do I feel as if I am not going to last?

I was only 22 when Christine, my wife-to-be, and I first lived together. We were in dire poverty but desperately in love. I was to start a matriculation course after the Christmas break. Sitting tight in the interim, our mutually excited biochemistry helped us while away the time.

That, and flicking through my collection of *The Face*. We shared an admiration for Leigh Bowery, Steve Strange and Martin Degville, as well as Jean Paul Gaultier's skirts/kilts for men and Kurt Cobain's occasional dress.

In the Queensland summer heat, I had taken to wearing beach towels around my waist; then when it got too hot, her sarongs. She gently suggested to me, 'If you want to wear a skirt or dress, I won't mind. I will love you no matter what'. Trepidation arrested my body. My tone, self-protective: 'I wouldn't do that.' Startled, she asked, 'Why ever not?'. Respiration halted and a spraining sensation up my spine, I reeled. 'Because I am a man.'

We were young, but there was genuine depth to our mutual intimacy and understanding. My response was absurdly disingenuous, utterly incongruent with every other way I behaved with her. Her invitation was out of love and care. But she could now see the fundamental distress it was baring; it was clear that any persistence would have been cruel.

For so long, I would only permit the most inert exploration of my gender. There was safety in being a passive observer, either of self or (increasingly) of my heroes. Only with the box lid closed. Every other way had resulted in loss or the threat of it. So would acting on her suggestion; I was certain of it.

My appreciation of queer culture must be at a distance. I was to be a normal, happily married man, no longer a confused loser who could never find their place, who could never get it right, a source of worry to the family. It was sweet of Christine to think I could be loved for who I am, but she was wrong. I would be shown the door.

I was working interstate, alone in my hotel room, exiled from the warmth of Christine and our daughter, at the behest and pleasure of my employer. Fat, Forty and Fired? If only! No, just fat and forty. Music television was playing in the background as self-solace, but my focus was on the laptop, not the TV screen. When Le Pie's 'Secrets' appeared, my attention was diverted, and I could not look away.

It's like Cilla Black backed by a grunge band. But why am I weeping? What is so poignant? Oh, that's Newtown! First all this work, and now this song is slowly killing me.

Solitude and tunes, walking and pensiveness, distinctly female self-surrender. It reflected a surrendering that I had avoided my whole life. I could not verbalise my unease during those late-night Newtown walks of my youth. Yet now, a disturbing notion: that I was once the young woman depicted on the screen. That, if I had been truly free, I would still have been blue and a little mislaid as she depicts; but at least I would have been.

Long-held suppressions now seemed dangerously close to faltering. Emotions crashing against cognition, crashing against contingency. *I am not going to last.*

I started wearing clear nail varnish, including at work, as if it would relieve the turmoil. My new boss thought I was weird. Was she a bigot, or was it just because I was weird? Either way, when I heard she was intending to 'manage me out of the business', I thought I could tough it out, and later leave on my own terms. However, each new stressor would amplify the fissures between my true identity and my corporal/corporate presence.

Once I broke, I was Broken, capable only of respite. On the Friday, my boss and I had a meeting where I openly cried and so was sent home. By the Saturday, I was in a foetal position, covered in my own tears and snot; too afraid to make a move in stark fear that it would be one to end my life. *I am not going to last.* Friends drove me to the ICU of a private psychiatric hospital. It was the ICU for weeks, followed by an open ward for months.

Between the hourly night checks, I would neither awake nor sleep. A barely discernible mental stirring emerged. Particles of this hypnagogic qualia, over a few days, bonded into a proto-thought. *I am/you are a girl, and you need to stop hiding me/you.* Over time, this culminated in a mental image of myself at around five years old in the dark, but in a dress. At times, she was aggravated, as I had not allowed her to 'go outside'. Stomping in the darkness, demanding illumination.

I am female and affirmed. I have named my girl, socially and legally. I am growing breasts and expanding my hips. Skirts, blouses, ponte pants, nail gloss and make-up abound. Life now seems easier. Not easy, just easier. I am going to last.

How many people have the opportunity to unpack their inner child from past trauma? I have finally opened the box flaps, reached out my arms and lifted my girl out. I cannot stop embracing her. Giggling and gorgeous, she is finally in the light.

As a loving dedication to the songs referenced in this work (and some that didn't make the '7-inch remix'), a Spotify playlist has been collated here:

EXCERPT FROM 'THE GRAPHENE PRAYER'

Geosmin Turpin

I've done enough quantum physics to know
That transitions still occur even when they are forbidden.
Love is the same thing as paying attention
And I am choosing to hear myself.

Too long have I starved myself of lilies
While trying to survive on bread
I don't want to be a bottle tree
Safe and dreaming
I'd be rather be free or…

The Capuchin monk said:

'I am inexorably devoured by the love of God, and the love of my neighbour'

So I'll hang out in the emergency room doing favours for people
While we're waiting for you to be seen by a doctor.
Because even if it's the fucking that got me here, today,
God I want it to be the laughter that takes me.

So let's show some
tenderness At the
interface between
you and I.

Let's braid our hair and watch *Ginger Snaps*
Because God save our broken little revenge-filled bodies,
I'm a bulldog of hot allostatic load and a strong bite
And you're a whale trying to drown your fears and save us
Whether from weeping at this absurdity or greeting it with laughter.

I thought this impulse was to
Tear everything to fucking pieces
Waging a black fax attack against the whole world
To ease the nausea of the Chiba city blues
I equipped my knife of never letting go and told myself
If the last person on Earth is a trans girl, then let it be me.

Turn loose my death rays and kill them all
A strontium dog seeing bodies where people should be
And from the ashes let me press graphene so clean
And pure
And sharp
It cleaves me into superconductive pieces
Like a moth drowning in lavender essence.

I eventually learnt that this impulse wasn't what I was feeling at all
I stopped chasing the glitches and messing up my save files
When I realised all those not saved would be lost
Instead I choose to reinvent
To introduce a second biological clock to change me
To walk through the dark and be reborn
Even when loving yourself is bitter work.

I escape that infinite feedback loop of my guts and electricity, statics and noise
I transcend. I forgive
Myself and those who hurt me
I put on my redemption mantle as I know that
That which is indefinable is divine.

NOBLE MAIDEN

Patterson Rainbird-Webb

There is something undeniable about this new aesthetic:
Barefoot and barely presentable
as I slow-dance in the kitchen at 3 am,
nobody but me, my shadow and a gentle grey kitten who patiently
watches me pour another cup of coffee.
I stir in cinnamon,
a taste that's heady and all too sweet against the roof of my mouth,
so strong it makes me want to gag.
And yet I sing under my breath:
old tunes I have no business remembering
and lullabies brought to me on the wind
[singing] all you have is fire
—and the place you have to reach.

My mother wanted a girl she could put together like a jigsaw,
a girl who would sit still and patiently endure
the effort it took to construct
the perfect plait, perfect updo,
perfect winged eyeliner, perfect blush,
perfect poise, perfect dress,
perfect daughter.
Instead she had me,
a muddled and confused thing
with a tangled mess of curls and eyes that couldn't quite look away.
Something with dirty fingers that knew the give and take of every
leaf and blade of grass,
something that couldn't sit still on creaking church pews,
because for all the beauty they pursued, she'd seen the unmatched
grace of rolling thunder
and the indisputable life of the ocean.
While other girls watched the boy chase the girl to a perfect kiss

she worshipped the women who took up their weapons and refused to keep their peace
—a child raised on a steady diet of Victorian poetry, Greek myth and poison. Stitched together with images of Artemis, Scottish women and a heathenish name.

My mother would lead me in prayer each night before bed, hoping against all hope to change what was in me. But my father made me wonder if I could be a knight one day, taught me to sing their vows of honour and justice during those ungodly hours when sleep was far.
The hours when his blood called to us both in its ancient tongue.
The hours where his stories became my bible. The hours when the smell of lemongrass and rain filled the house.
The hours when I would be barefoot and dancing in the kitchen, barely presentable yet undeniably free.

LIKE CRYINGS

Elwin Schok

ache like liquid
nitrogen nerves

retching through green dawns,
frost screams
quivery like cryings

i've been embroidering butterfly
wings on my sternum and also my body
is a thousand shards of honey and also
i am stitched onto the inside of a geranium in the snow

COMPLETENESS

Elwin Schok

beginning with: growing slowly into a body
fibres arranging themselves gracefully and
the morning tuned so beautifully
to precipitate erupting into limbs
upon waking—we sleep
like speckled cats. there isn't a lot of sense even
in physicality. I've been piecing together
fragments of self, held
like archaeological porcelain

outlines. completeness suggested

like archaeological porcelain
fragments of self, held
in physicality. I've been piecing together pieces
like speckled cats. there isn't a lot of sense even
upon waking—we sleep
to precipitate erupting into limbs
the morning tuned so beautifully
fibres arranging themselves gracefully and
beginning with: growing slowly into a body

Afterword

Trans and gender-diverse people face many barriers to writing. Growing up queer, living with minority stress, social stigma and punitive shame can show up in the mind and body as trauma, depression, anxiety, pain and chronic illness. Creative practice also requires leisure, social and cultural capital and peers. Many of the contributors to this book have noted how lack of formal training, lack of community and lack of time—between working and surviving—impact their ability to write.

A publishing industry controlled by people who are overwhelmingly white, middle-class and cisgendered is hard to break into and limits writing to the expectations of the mainstream. This book is a record of those who have found a way—by seeking and building their own peer connections and communities, by sharing their work and the work of others.

Yet, as we name our struggles, we also remember those who did not survive the discrimination, neglect and violence to which trans bodies, and particularly black and brown trans bodies, are subject. Provision of government funding for gender-diverse community and cultural activities is a response to statistics of suffering. Thus, there is a connection between the enabling conditions of this writing and those gender-diverse folk in our histories and communities who did not and do not have such opportunities. Being able to write is a privilege, and survivors' guilt underlies the production of this collection.

There is no adequate way to represent those whose stories have not been told without symbolic violence. We cannot know about other people what they cannot tell us themselves. In the absence of their words, we invite you to pause and ask: *What other histories would we have needed to ensure the survival and flourishing of the most vulnerable and marginalised within our communities?*

The contributors

a. t. green

a. t. green is a non-binary, autistic spoonie with a tenuous connection with time. They are currently studying social work and help to run the monthly poetry gathering, To the Ends of the Verse. They throw most of their poems onto Instagram (@riotmeds) and spend the rest of their time creating rude cross-stitch projects. They will always get confused by tense and have just leaned into it at this stage.

Adele Aria

Braised and warmed in clay pots and histories, Adele is shaped by a voracious curiosity and appetite for adventure and wrestling questions. Standing deliberately and inevitably beyond many boundaries, they hope to keep learning, disrupting, insisting on possible futures through creative non-fiction, poetic, performance, and academic writing found in international and Australian publications. Adele navigates collective narrative and actions with queer love and body named as disabled in an ableist space.

I pay respect to the Indigenous custodianship and survival of the unceded lands upon which I've been thankful to live after forced displacements.

Adrik Kemp

I am a cis gay man; however I wrote this creative non-fiction piece as a collaboration with one of my best friends of more than 20 years, who is trans. He asked me to write it with him and submit it under my name, as he is Lebanese and needs to remain anonymous. Personally, I am a published author of various short stories and novellas, with a focus on the LGBTQ+ experience.

Alex Lee

Alex Lee (they/them) is the functional name for a more or less coherent and contingent cluster of experiences that embody as transgender, queer, white settler and chronically ill. They love to dream up creative and critical interventions with other queer folk.

Bron 'Richo' Richardson

Richo is a queer, trans man currently living on the unceded lands of the Wurundjeri people. He served in the Australian Army from 2014–18 and has recently made a submission to the Royal Commission into Defence and Veteran Suicide.

David Azul

David Azul (they/them) is a writer and academic (who would love to be a DJ, skater and multimedia artist). They live and work on unceded Dja Dja Wurrung country. David is interested in challenging the practice of classifying humans and other beings into kinds and art into genres and works on imagining and experimenting with alternatives.

Eliot Jane Walton

Eliot Jane Walton is an emerging writer and aspiring lesbian based in Melbourne. She is a voracious consumer of carbon ring structures and is completing her PhD in experimental particle physics at Monash University. You can find her work, both poetry and prose, in *Gems Zine*, *Lot's Wife*, *Verge: Uncanny* and the student publication *Incisors & Grinders*.

Elwin Schok

Elwin Schok lives on Wurundjeri land and works across artistic and academic mediums. Their writing engages with language and the body and has appeared in *Bent Street*, *Voiceworks* and *Above Water*.

Finnley Stirling

I'm Finnley and I use they/them pronouns. I identify as queer and nonbinary and am 23, living in Naarm. I'm sparkly and colourful, I love reading and my superpower is empathy. I'm passionate about storytelling and am an advocate for young people, diversity and inclusion and my community.

Geosmin Turpin

Geosmin is a poet-scientist and a trans fem neurodyke, who named herself after the molecule responsible for the smell of rain. She holds a PhD in chemistry, in which she studied the boundary issues of nanoparticles. They believe all research is me-search and that chemistry is the poetry of matter.

Hailey McKenzie

I'm a 30-year-old proud Yorta Yorta woman. I'm trans and have been out for four years now. I'm a struggling writer, doing what I can while also trying to put food on the table.

Hester J. Rook

Hester J. Rook is an Australian Shadows Award-winning and Rhysling Award-short-listed poet and fiction writer and is co-editor of *Twisted Moon Magazine*. They are often found salt-scrunched on beaches, reading arcane tales and losing the moon in mugs of tea. Find Hester on Twitter @hesterjrook and read more poems and fiction at https://hesterjrook.com.

Isabelle Quilty

Isabelle Quilty (she/they) is a non-binary writer and poet from regional New South Wales, Australia. Most of their work is based around LGBTQ+ topics, working towards a greener future and inspired by their South Asian ancestry. They've been published by a variety of magazines including *Spineless Wonders, Kindling and Sage,*

Mascara Literary Review and *Demure* magazine. They also have a bachelor's degree in writing and publishing and love a good oat milk iced latte. Currently, they're working on their first short story collection, *The Dead Flower Society*.

Jes Layton

Jes Layton (he/him, she/her) invented writing, the aeroplane and the internet. He was also the first person to reach the North Pole. Jes is a writer, content creator and artist who works and lives on Wurundjeri land. His written work can be found in *SBS Voices*, *Junkee*, *Voiceworks*, *Kill Your Darlings*, *Archer*, *The Victorian Writer* and scattered elsewhere online and in print. She has short stories published in *Underdog: #LoveOzYA Short Stories* (Nero, 2019) and *Growing Up in Country Australia* (Black Inc., 2022. Jes has also presented work at a variety of writers festivals and is the 2022 digital manager for the National Young Writers' Festival, admin for ClimbingQTs and marketing and communications coordinator for Express Media. His tweets have been written about in *Teen Vogue*, the *Daily Mail*, *Screen Rant*, *BuzzFeed* and more. Exposure was apparently payment.

Jordie Slonim

Jordie is a 49-year-old trans, queer, genderqueer human, currently writing a memoir. Their lifelong exploration of the corporeal in relation to the spiritual is central to their writing style. They grew up as a dancer and choreographer and now work as a kinesiologist and kinesiology teacher.

Jules Joy

Jules Joy is a non-binary trans woman, writer, speaker and trans educator living and generally trying to make sense of life in Naarm.

Kai Ash

I am a trans autistic writer. Based on Jagera country (Brisbane region), I have been shortlisted for the Ampersand Prize 2022, the Adaptable program 2022, the Lane Cove Literary Awards 2021 and the Lord Mayor's Creative Writing Awards 2020. I am a 2022 mentee in the ASA/CA Award Mentorships Program.

Kashindi Shabani Gady

Kashindi Shabani Gady is the executive secretary of Savie Asbl NGO LGBT PGEL, in Bukavu, Democratic Republic of Congo.

Louis Blake

I am a transgender man living on Wurundjeri/Boonwurrung land. I love being in nature, especially on Djab Wurrung and Jardwadjali country. Respect to the custodians of these lands. Sovereignty was never ceded.

Madison Godfrey

Madison 'Maddie' Godfrey is a writer, editor and educator who lives on Whadjuk Noongar land with a rescue cat named Sylvia. They have performed poetry at the Sydney Opera House, the Royal Albert Hall, St Paul's Cathedral, TEDx and Glastonbury Festival. Madison is a previous recipient of the Kat Muscat Fellowship, the Varuna Poetry Flagship Fellowship and the 2021 Propel Youth Arts WA Creative Contribution Award. Currently they are completing a PhD on prose poetry and wearing a lot of purple. Their forthcoming book, *Dress Rehearsals*, will be published by Allen & Unwin under Nakkiah Lui's imprint, Joan, in March 2023. ' Multiple Choice' previously appeared in *Australian Poetry Journal*, volume 12.1, 'Divergence, Relevance' (Australian Poetry, 2022). www.maddiegodfrey.com

Madison Moffat

Madison Moffat is a trans woman whose relationship between themselves and their writing pen is typically one of guilt. Very occasionally, this is overcome; much to her pleasure. Years ago, she wrote the occasional short stage play, and performed at an event called Scene that was held at Revolver Upstairs. She also previously dabbled in critique, as a regular contributor to Melbourne's *Theatre Press* review website. She is based in Naarm (Melbourne).

Mohammad Taha

My name is Mohammad. I am a non-binary person of colour under the trans umbrella. I am many things: a migrant, a scientist, a stranger without a home, reader, writer, soon to be filmmaker and an advocate for the queer people of colour. I have grief and joy in my heart in a constant battle that I'd rather write than talk to people about. One last thing: when I'm walking I practise improvised monologues so I can have a speech to defend a sister in holy queerness.

Nick Lawson

Nick (they/he) is a fiercely unapologetic intersectional humanitarian, world builder and storyteller living on Wathaurong land.

paki aoraki pehi

paki was born in Aotearoa/New Zealand and currently lives and creates in Naarm/Melbourne. paki's work has been acquired by the National Gallery of Australia, the National Gallery of Victoria, the Art Gallery of South Australia and public and private collections nationally and internationally. paki held the solo exhibitions *Unauthenticated* at Blak Dot Gallery in 2019 and *Dark Sepia* at Incinerator Gallery in 2020 and in 2021 was a finalist for the Blake Prize.

Patterson Rainbird-Webb

I am an autistic individual on the non-binary spectrum. I am currently studying towards my second degree in computer science and act as the media manager for UP&OUT, the queer society on my campus. Along with writing, coding and illustrating, I spend a lot of time learning more about the world around me.

Rowan Heath

Rowan Heath is a writer and editor living on Wurundjeri land. They have a master's degree in publishing and communications from the University of Melbourne. Their writing has appeared in *Verge* and *Antithesis*, and they're one of the duo behind the podcast *Of the Devil's Party*.

Sadie St James

Sadie St James is a multidisciplinary artist with a passion for writing and performing poetry. She has been writing spoken word poetry since 2014. The pieces included in this book are taken from a series of self-published poetry anthologies.

Sarah L

Sarah L is a transgender woman navigating the currents of geography, culture and gender. She is a wordsmith fluent in machine and human languages.

Shea Martin

Shea Martin (they/she) is a secondary school teacher, DJ and reality television fanatic. Their writing is an invitation to the laugh riot at the intersection of neurodiversity, queerness, transness and sobriety, delivered in an ornamental box full of sedated butterflies. *The First Transgendered Housewife* is their inaugural effort to convert the queer masses to the Church of Latter Day Bravolebrities.

Shreya Tekumalla

Shreya was born in 2002 in India, but for practical purposes considers himself a first-generation Indian-Australian. He came out to his family as transgender at 18 years old and is hoping to medically transition sometime in the near future. He's currently studying for a career in medicine, and if not studying or writing, he's probably playing horror video games (despite his being a massive coward).

Son Vivienne

Son identifies as multiplicity—parent, permaculturalist, pansexual, genderqueer and non-binary. Their lived experience includes neurodivergence and chronic illness, and they are from white, working-class origins in regional Australia. They have a background as a media writer/director/producer, including bilingual short films and animations in Vietnamese and Adnyamathanha. They have a PhD in cultural studies exploring queer online activism, privacy and publicness, and they are currently finishing a book titled *Queering Safe Spaces: Being Brave Beyond Binaries*. They are general manager at Transgender Victoria, a community-led not for profit advocating for gender-diverse wellbeing and peer support. Their less verbose, more embodied projects include cultivating abundance in their garden and generosity in their children. More info at Son's website: www.incitestories.com.au.

The Swamp System

We are an OSDD system who are a gaggle of trans goblins!

Tiff Tan

My name is Tiff. I was supposed to be born as a boy, and at ages four and five disliked to wear a skirt. No matter how my mum forced me, I woudn't wear one. I made noise and cried. I am one of five siblings—three brothers and one sister and me. I don't have the rights and freedom to talk about LGBTIQA in my hometown, a small village. I wanted to have a secure life like others LGBTIQA+, to have a community and people around to support trans people no matter where they come from. When I was a little kid, at that time I was unable to share my feelings and my problem with family and friends, because I didn't want to make them afraid and stressed by my gender diversity. I just kept it for myself for 30 years. After, I came to Australia, only to be able to talk and share my stories openly.

Tobi Evans

Tobi Evans (he/they) is a feral queer academic and social justice doula living in Naarm (Melbourne). He has a PhD in cultural studies and has published award-winning research on masculinity and violence in popular culture. His first book, *Reimagining Masculinity and Violence in* Game of Thrones *and* A Song of Ice and Fire, was published in 2022. He currently makes trouble in local government, working towards gender equality, LGBTIQA* inclusion and disability justice.

Thank you...

Thank you to the many people who worked with us to make this project possible:

- Sam Elkin for his tireless advocacy for trans and gender-diverse folks, and in particular for initiating this project;
- Marcel Liemant for bringing his fiction-writing excellence to our workshops;
- Gordon Thompson for generously sharing his expertise in publishing and book design;
- paki aoraki pehi for permission to reproduce the wonderful linocut print that graces our cover;
- Aspen Beilharz for gently guiding the writers in curating and preparing their spoken word performance;
- Jessica Bellamy at the City of Maribyrnong for providing us with our gorgeous launch venue, the Bluestone Church Arts Space;
- Hayley Lawson at Footscray Community Arts Centre for the use of their beautiful studio workshop space;
- The Shed for promotional resources;
- The amazing gender-diverse creatives of this project, who made together the 'supportive, learning, opening, expanding environment' that we all needed 'to keep returning to the writing and growing'—to borrow the words of one contributor;
- You, the reader, for engaging these writings—may they stay with you;

* And finally, all the trans and gender-diverse folk who have come before us, and all those with whom we share this time.

We say thanks to the weirdos, the lost souls, the revolutionaries, the visionaries, the wild children, the healers, the dreamers, the creators, the intuitives, the way-seers, the lovers, the fighters, the beaten, the broken and the damned, the intersectional, the nerds, the queers and all those who love them.

Thanks for your stories and music unheard, your art and writings unseen and your names unknown.

We do not want to see the histories of generation after generation slip away.

Let us build each other up, lead by example and challenge the social norms.

About this project

This project was initiated by Sam Elkin (Spilling the T Collective) and funded by the City of Maribyrnong and was produced by A Thousand Threads. It included writing workshops and peer editing and mentoring sessions, collaborative editorial work, spoken word performance development and creation of the book you are reading now.

Spilling the T Collective is a peer-led trans and gender-diverse writers collective founded by Sam Elkin and Yves Rees. Its facilitators connect emerging writers with their community across Australia. The group provides peer support, feedback and mentoring as members workshop new pieces and share ideas.

A Thousand Threads is a collaborative, ongoing writing initiative for trans, genderqueer and non-binary folk, peer-led and designed by Alex Nichols with Urszula Dawkins. Its focus is collaborative storytelling, community building and peer support through words-based creative practice.

Spilling the T Collective and A Thousand Threads were both initially supported by Transgender Victoria's SPARK program.

Any profit gained from the sale of this book will be donated to organisations directly supporting trans and gender-diverse communities.

Lightning Source UK Ltd.
Milton Keynes UK
UKHW050842071222
413405UK00012BA/129

9 780645 42942